Beyoncé Biography

"The Queen of Music and Unstoppable Fame"

Herlind Gonzalez

BEYONCÉ
BIOGRAPHY

The Queen of Music and Unstoppable Fame

CONTENTS

CHAPTER 1
Beyoncé Is the Greatest Performer Alive, According to Beychella. I'm not debating.

CHAPTER 2
On the Road Together

CHAPTER 3
Jay-Z's apology to Beyoncé is more than just gossip—it's a political act.

CHAPTER 4
All Her Single Ladies

CHAPTER 5
The Elevator

CHAPTER 6
The Art of Being Beyoncé

CHAPTER 7
Grown Women: A Conversation with an Icon About Coming of Age

CHAPTER 8
What Queen Bey Means to Everyone

CHAPTER 9
Beyoncé, Influencer

CHAPTER 10
The King of Pop and the Queen of AI

CHAPTER 11
Beyoncé the Fearless

CHAPTER 12
Living into the Lemonade: Redefining Black Women's Spirituality in Beyoncé's Era

CHAPTER 13
Beyoncé's Radical Ways

CHAPTER 14
La Reina can be found in Queen Bey

CHAPTER 15
Style So Sacred

CHAPTER 16
Beyoncé's Radiance

CHAPTER 17
Because Beyoncé

CHAPTER 18
King Bey

CHAPTER 19
Beyoncé's Southern Origins and References

CHAPTER 20
B & V: A Love Letter

INTRODUCTION:
What Might a Black Girl Be in This World?

I first heard of Beyoncé in the late 1990s. I was a rookie editor at Newsweek magazine, and one of my responsibilities included writing about music. My Brooklyn Heights apartment was like my own Barbie Dream House: top floor of a brownstone, incredibly high ceilings, two levels—living room and kitchen on the first floor, loft bedroom and alcove on the second. My L.A. buddies all got keys to my apartment. On my couch, my friend John Singleton drafted his remake of Shaft. My friend Cassandra, who lived in California, and I used to FedEx clothes back and forth for big gatherings a decade or so before companies like eBay and Rent the Dress. I've attended and thrown some absolutely incredible parties.

Women in modern R&B had a golden era. I'd construct playlists with all of my favorites, such as Mariah Carey's "Breakdown" with Krayzie Bone and Wish Bone from Bone Thugs-N-Harmony. "Are You That Somebody?" by Aaliyah. Every Missy Elliott song, every Erykah Badu song from her womynist debut. Deborah Cox's "Nobody's Supposed to Be Here." Vanessa Williams' song "Colors of the Wind." Toni Braxton can sing about anything. Destiny's Child, particularly that early Wyclef Jean remix—because Lauryn Hill was the queen of hip hop back then—were simple to incorporate into the mix. Destiny's Child's "Independent Women" was a game changer. The 2001 song was used as the theme song for a Charlie's Angels remake starring Drew Barrymore, Cameron Diaz, and Lucy Liu. There had been several personnel changes in Destiny's Child. Rumor had it that there had been quite a bit of drama behind the scenes.

By 2001, however, there was no disputing that Destiny's Child—reformed as a trio with Beyoncé firmly at the helm—was pure fire. In the "Independent Women" video, Beyoncé at the head of a boardroom table was everything I—and every young woman I knew—wanted to be: gorgeous, in charge, with her best girls by her side. Beyoncé 1.0 had come, and the way she held the camera's gaze made us feel as if we were all invited to her party. The fire in her belly, the almost unearthly amount of focus and ambition in her eyes, are what make Beyoncé so clearly Beyoncé.

Growing up as an Afro-Latina in America, in a society rife with continuous reminders of race and prejudice, I've spent my whole life asking and answering one question: what may a Black girl be in this world? Beyoncé Knowles-Carter's great body of work appears to me to be an answer to that issue as well. What exactly is a Black female in this world? Everything—and even more than you could have imagined. Beyoncé's place, her work as a marker and reflection of power and promise, will be undeniable when the history of Black women in the twenty-first century is recorded. She is more than a pop sensation. Her omnipresence implies she is constantly at the crossroads of intersectionality.

I married the love of my life in 2002. It had been a whirlwind relationship, in my opinion. After seven months of dating, he proposed. A year later, we married. I was invited to teach at Bowdoin College in Maine three months after we married. My spouse remained at our New York apartment. But he flew up to see me three out of four weekends. I'd drive from my little riverside cottage in Woolwich to Portland and pick him up at the airport. What exactly is a Black female in this world? Anything and everything she could have dreamt.

Growing up on Ocean Avenue in Brooklyn, I never pictured myself in Maine, spending tranquil afternoons by the Atlantic Ocean swapping my recycling for a handful of wrinkled one dollar notes, enough money to buy fresh lobsters from fishermen at the pier. I never dreamed growing up in Brooklyn in the '80s, listening to

Héctor Lavoe and Run DMC, that I'd be shaking hands with rugged New England fishermen.

In the 2000s, it became evident that Beyoncé's one-name appellation was well earned. Beyoncé was as much a part of music as Sting, Prince, Michael, or Bono. My attention was drawn to her in 2010, when she slammed the pause button on everything. Her mother had suggested that she take a break, and she did so, taking nearly a year off to "live life, to be inspired by things again." She traveled and occasionally revisited all of the locations she never got to see while on tour, including museums and ballet performances, Glastonbury (as a spectator, not a performer), the Great Wall of China, and Australia. She stated in an Essence article:

Visiting a country without an itinerary was so appealing to me. After a few days in Auckland, New Zealand, for the start of my husband's tour, I settled in Australia for five weeks ... I had no schedule while taking in the sites of Melbourne, Brisbane, Perth and my favorite Aussie city, Sydney. They have the best restaurants and the harbor is awesome. It was a carefree existence for me ... In London I met Sade, one of my favorite artists. I've loved and admired her for so long. In Russia I found vintage jewelry and saw the ballet Swan Lake. But what is being abroad without enjoying the food? All over Italy the streets smell like gelato. In Paris my nephew Julez and I had escargot for lunch and it was actually tasty (though not as good as a funnel cake at the Houston Rodeo). In Capri I ate pizza and drank red wine every Sunday ... I'm drawn to the ocean. Whether it's jumping from a yacht (those photos drive my mother crazy; she thinks it's dangerous), swimming, snorkeling in the Red Sea (I've never seen fish so breathtaking), or just walking on the sand, the sea has a calming effect on me. Croatia has the most beautiful water—although it's the saltiest I ever tasted. I floated on my back for close to an hour in the Mediterranean Sea. It was one of the best moments of my life.

For me, it was a wow moment when Beyoncé became synonymous with another word: power. Even at the highest echelons of entertainment, there appears to be an incessant, even cruel, push to keep creating, to stay in the game, lest you fall even further down the pop cultural food chain.

Beyoncé's hiatus meant a lot to me because it felt like she was saying, "I have no doubt or concern about staying on top." She was engaged in her own game. She was making up her own regulations. While it would be some time before she crowned herself Queen Bey (and, on occasion, King Bey), I believe her 2010 absence was her first fully autonomous move. She later sang in her song "Pretty Hurts" about striving to win the crown without falling. But the sabbatical, the time she spent away from the spotlight, showed that she had quietly and confidently climbed to monarchy at the age of 30. She wasn't just another pop princess anymore. She was a queen in her chosen sector, and she would wear the crown for the rest of her life.

Brittney Cooper, who declared Beyoncé to be her feminist inspiration, talks about why Jay-Z's apology on 4:44 is so important to all women, but especially Black women. I love how Emmy-winning writer/actor/producer Lena Waithe shares her personal perspective on growing up in Generation Beyoncé, as well as how YouTube star Kid Fury recalls practicing Beyoncé dance routines in his childhood bedroom and discusses what Beyoncé means to the homosexual community. Isabel González Whitaker discusses the significance of Beyoncé singing in Spanish, as well as how the Venn diagram of where Southern culture and Latinx culture intersect is larger than we realize: It doesn't get more Latin than devotion to lip gloss and a mother's rage at leaving the house undone. "When you look at beauty and the Southern black girl, it can be indistinguishable from beauty as presented in Dominican or Cuban culture," says Zandria Robinson, an Africana Studies expert. "There is a shared emphasis on beauty, elegance, femininity, and self-presentation." Michael Eric Dyson writes a sincere, dramatic examination of Beyoncé and Michael Jackson's creative connection, and why he believes she has exceeded the King of Pop. Not every author in this collection is a die-hard devotee. Melissa Harris-Perry and her former student Mankaprr Conteh argue about Beyoncé, addressing everything from colorism to class politics. And there's a lot more.

Beyoncé and Jay-Z have just published their video for "Apesh*t," which was shot in the Louvre, as I write this. The Louvre video hit home because France in general, and Paris in particular, have long been a part of my story. Beyoncé Giselle Knowles has worked so hard for so long that she is deserving of a serious, in-depth examination of her life and work. She's still quite young. She'll be 37 years old when this book comes out. Despite this, her career path has more than 25 years ahead of her. It occurred to me that we were watching Bey dance, pose, and sing her way through the Louvre while we were putting the finishing touches on this book. This collection of writings is almost like a museum retrospective of Beyoncé's solar system. Beyoncé has repeatedly stated that she has no intention of distancing herself from the challenge of being a Black woman in this world. That struggle, on the other hand, is a bass line in her music, one that echoes in her pride in being one of us, the highs and lows of our collective invention and creativity.

"I come from a lineage of broken male-female relationships, abuse of power, and mistrust," she said in the September 2018 issue of Vogue. That was the only way I was able to address the difficulties in my own relationship. We are both scared and beautiful because we are connected to the past and know our history." Allow those final few words to soak in for a moment: "bruised and beautiful." This book, on the other hand, reminds us that hers is a distinctly American story of a girl born in Texas who formed a vision of womanhood that has affected men and women of all generations all over the world. It's about a young woman who slowly and confidently invented the power she needed to be free. What exactly is a Black female in this world? She may one day rule over everything. Queen Bey, we salute you.

CHAPTER 1
Beyoncé Is the Greatest Performer Alive, According to Beychella. I'm not debating.

House Knowles' Beyoncé Giselle. Her first name. Edges snatcher. Stage Assassin. Creole Wonderland resident. Black Girl of Legend. Queen. I need to increase my Biotin consumption and reorder my Jamaican Black Castor Oil. Beyoncé is still coming for my new growth. I'm not even mad since I'd gladly give up my hair for the Queen. I didn't attend Coachella, but I was a Beychella citizen, watching her performance and recognizing that we were witnessing a legend.

That is not an exaggeration. Beyoncé has already gained icon status if she decides she's tired of us lessers and never releases another piece of music, and I'm not here to argue with you. People have been designated as icons for doing and being less. But this woman, who has created history time and again, including being the first Black woman to headline Coachella, seized the opportunity to solidify her reputation as the greatest entertainer alive. She sang the Black national anthem with a 100-person all-Black band behind her, giving her everything she had. In the tradition of traditionally Black Greek letter fraternities and sororities, they performed a full step show while wearing branded hoodies. She played for two hours for a predominantly white Coachella audience, with relatively few white faces on stage. But in reality, she was performing for the millions of Black people she knew who were watching online from all around the world. It was an outstanding performance. It was a brave display. It was a Broadway musical that I would watch over and over again.

I recall when Lemonade was released and how it was a salute to diasporic Blackness. The fact that she is so dedicated to paying genuine honor to her Blackness, Africanness, and diaspora makes my spirit shoki and azonto. Furthermore, she does it on such large scales that she ensures the world consumes her pride. To prepare fans for all that Nubian, Lemonade had Bey rock some braids with baby hair. She used women with various hairstyles throughout the film. There are righteous afros, beautiful weaves and braids, and an army of ancestral blessings standing around. But it was Bey's devotion to Afro-spiritualism that stood out the most in that Black-ass video.

Your ears were overwhelmed as your eyes danced along with Bey and her crew because she also sounded her finest. We were witnessing the greatest of a living legend. Six months after giving birth to twins. She never appeared tired. She danced and sang at full throttle for two hours. She is amazing. I've never had children, and I performed a karaoke rendition of Sister Act 2's "Joyful, Joyful." I spent four minutes two-stepping and lip syncing. I stepped off the stage and had to take a ten-minute break to collect my breath.

That's why I've spent so much of today battling with people online. This performance seems to have pushed me past the point of no return in my fandom. I've always admired Beyoncé. I buy every album. But I hadn't been a Beyhive member. I hadn't been hauling people for her. That is no longer the case. I just paid my membership fees. At the next meeting, I'll bring Flaming Hots.

HOW CAN ANYONE DISREGARD THIS WOMAN'S ABILITY?!?! People tried it today, and my patience has run out. How can you look at what she does and say, "meh?" It's ridiculous at this point. Here's the deal. I'm not suggesting that people make Beyoncé the queen of their hearts. However, the woman is EXCELLENT. People go to incredible lengths to disparage her excellence. When you spend hours every day, for 25 years, honing your skill. And you turn up and give it your all. You also respect your culture. And even when you turn up for individuals that look like you, folks might be all "MEH."

All I know is that Beychella has influenced the crap out of me. This woman is at the top, but she still acts as if each performance is her first and last. She acts as if she still has to impress people (as if this is her first time), and she leaves everything on the stage as if it's the final time we'll see her. She's always trying to outdo herself because she's not competing with anyone but herself. She doesn't take her position at the top for granted, which makes me admire her talent, humanity, and work ethic more than anything else. I will celebrate her accomplishments and scoff at anyone who attempts to belittle what she has accomplished. YES. I AM NOW OFFICIALLY AVAILABLE TO DRAG PERSONS WHO DO NOT AGREE. She inspires me to be a Black girl. And I'm proud to claim that a Black lady is the best entertainer alive. P.S. So... Here's my Beyhive membership kit. Is it possible to get it using pins? I need to wear it with my jackets. Please send me a T-shirt in an extra-small size.

CHAPTER 2
On the Road Together

I was in junior high when Destiny's Child debuted their first music video, "No, No, No." I remember seeing this unusual kind of Black girl, one we hadn't seen before, with my buddies, all the Black girls. Beyoncé was a Black queen as well. I saw Diana Ross and Lena Horne in it and thought, "So that's what beauty is." That's what being hot entails. That is what it means to take the lead. I also felt compelled to shield her, as if she were a friend. Years after seeing her play with Michelle and Kelly at Chicago's House of Blues, when she released her first solo album, I remember thinking, Oh man, I hope this is good.

I was worried about her because I adored Destiny's Child in all of its incarnations and didn't want any of its fame or strength to fade away. Of course, it didn't; instead, it grew. In some ways, we're all on the same path as Beyoncé. I recall her being so self-assured and emerging into her own womanhood. In my twenties, I moved to Los Angeles in search of my own self-confidence and womanhood. That's when I started listening to her songs and relating to her journey in terms of figuring out who I was as a woman, a person, and a Black woman. And today, especially where I am in my career and looking at her, I realize the need for a baptism in which you bless yourself with water and ordain yourself a new woman. Only then can you take the first step. I've been thinking about her problems as I've gone through my own, and she gives you permission to stumble a little bit but then produce something beautiful out of that stumble. She demonstrates that you can survive like a phoenix no matter what life throws at you.

When Beyoncé's self-titled album came out, I fell in love with him. I wanted to feel the passion and connection to someone she talked about in that record. Lemonade is an album that pulls us all up. She discusses surviving heartbreak and betrayal with Lemonade. There's something so human and brave about it. It's also the record that represents community, as she includes all of her idols, such as Serena Williams.

Beyoncé utilized Lemonade to shed a light on a community of women of color, telling their tales and sharing their adventures. And just because Beyonce didn't win a Grammy for best album for Lemonade doesn't mean people won't listen to it. People wouldn't feel any less attached to Master of None if I hadn't won an Emmy for the Thanksgiving episode. Black women have traditionally served as the foundation of everything. Black women have never taken a back seat. Beyoncé demonstrates that we're all made of the same substance and that we're all in the same boat. She makes it her business to say things like, "I'm a mother, a wife, an activist, a daughter, and a friend." Even if we're not the same, we're all pals in this life. And she tells us that no matter how big or tiny our voices are, we must stand tall because our forefathers did. So who are we to say we can't do it? It makes no difference who you are, where you come from, or what your means are. Look at how she defends her feelings for Houston. I'm from Chicago, and while both cities have flaws, we know there is beauty in these cities that others may dismiss.

Beyoncé represents a light at the end of the tunnel for gay people. She may not be homosexual, but she, like Cher and Madonna, is a gay ally and idol in the community because she understands what it means to be different and to be unafraid of that fact. She speaks to individuals all around the world—gay, straight, trans, Black, white—because she can bridge all barriers. In this sense, she is related to Whitney Houston and Michael Jackson. They were proud African Americans who spoke to Black audiences, but they couldn't help but flow over to other audiences because they were so pure and special.

There's also the uniqueness of Beyoncé's work—her songs and her heart—that has propelled her. As a writer who writes about my own life, I know directly that detail attracts a larger audience.

I grew up listening to Whitney, Michael, and Prince. We may have lost them, but Beyoncé is not scared to carry on their talent and impact. I was watching Being Bobby Brown at the time, and Whitney was in the car when they started talking about Beyoncé. Whitney was offering her permission in a way. She was essentially saying, "Beyoncé, take it from here." I'm reminded of this every time I see Beyoncé. Whitney touched her, signaling her to proceed, a touch that indicated, "You got it from here."

CHAPTER 3
Jay-Z's apology to Beyoncé is more than just gossip—it's a political act.

Many critics have focused on 4:44's capitalist message, but Jay-Z's emotional admissions are extremely important to Black women. With the release of 4:44, black men of the hip hop generation are experiencing their Lemonade moment. By "Lemonade moment," I mean the cultural reckoning made possible by Beyoncé's April 2016 publication of her successful album Lemonade.

Beyoncé opened up about her troubles with her husband Jay-Z's infidelity, her father's adultery with her mother, and how impossible it is to persuade a man who is treating you badly to love you right on the album. Jay apologizes to Beyoncé and all the ladies he's damaged due to his immaturity on 4:44's title single. As someone who has experienced heartbreak at the hands of Black males, I thought the apology to be a breath of fresh air. Apologies from Black men to Black women are important. Relationships are difficult. Black partnerships are more difficult. This is not because African-Americans are more broken or disordered than any other group. No, we are not. But we grow up in a world that tells us otherwise. Black people have frequently had to scale steep mountains to find our way to each other, shaped by racism and its multigenerational assault on Black families.

Hip hop music and culture have been main spaces for Generation X and millennial Black people to sort out their relational expectations and worries about how men and women are supposed to act in romantic relationships since the late 1970s. All of these expectations about correct femininity and masculinity performances—about men as providers and women as recipients of that provision—are strongly molded not only by the continuing impacts of racism, but also by the sexism that pervades American culture. Hip hop, although giving Black men a voice about how they struggle to engage in the aforementioned patriarchal dream, also fostered the worst aspects of toxic masculinity, portraying Black men as emotionally unavailable, violent, hypersexed, immature, and rigid. Jay-Z's songs "Big Pimpin'" and "Girls, Girls, Girls" are only two examples from his extensive discography that highlight these themes.

On 4:44, Jay-Z removes the mask of Black male impenetrability by accepting full responsibility for the near-dissolution of his marriage to Beyoncé, this generation's greatest cultural symbol. He truly owns his stuff, as any decent apology should. Jay-Z admits in it that he built a relationship with Beyoncé that was like a "big mansion with cracks in it." To stay together, they had to demolish this metaphorical mansion and start again. Jay claims that ripping down and reconstructing is the most difficult thing he's ever done, even more difficult than surviving the violence of being fired at during his famed days as a drug dealer in Brooklyn.

Following the release of the album, there has been a flood of think pieces from Black men and women struggling with the ramifications of Jay-Z's revelations. I've found that Black males have mostly concentrated on the economic principles that Jay-Z raps about, but Black women have primarily focused on the significance of his confession and how his maltreatment of Beyoncé mimics Black women's more general difficulties with Black men. But, last we checked, there's only one person on the planet who has to believe Hov in real life, and as clever as the scenes-from-a-marriage gambit proved to ensure a boffo opening week, the true focus of this terse and finely composed, fiercely quotable album lies more in politics than romance." And these politics continue hip hop's long relationship with Black economic nationalism. Black scholars like Booker T. Washington have contended since the late 1800s that economic power is the route to Black emancipation. Jay-Z appears to believe in this concept, especially on the tune "Legacy," where he says, "generational wealth—that's the key." Because my parents don't have anything, that change began with me."

But Tate must be aware that Jay-Z is obsessed with money, in part because he wants to impress women. This is true for the vast majority of straight guys in capitalist America. Jigga feels secure enough now that he is worth nearly 10 figures to pursue other questions and to rethink his own fascination with showy consumption. What effect does America's fixation with money have on the quality of the relationships we cherish the most? Perhaps debating the virtues of Jay's money thinking is easier than dealing with the murkier realm of sentiments and responsibility for relational failures. However, Jay utilizes his mother, wife, and daughter Blue as a type of moral compass to remind him of what the purpose of the money, and the "legacy," should and will be. And, with the recent arrival of the twins Sir Carter and Rumi Knowles-Carter, these considerations of legacy have become even more relevant.

Some Black guys just claim that Jay-Z's apology is nothing new and that he does not go far enough. These men think his apology is a little late and not very impressive. To be sure, Black males apologizing in popular culture is not a new phenomenon. The Knowles-Carters are hip hop's First Couple, only slightly less important to Black people under 35 than the Obamas. They've been meaning to explain for a long time. Jay-Z also apologizes for the Solange incident, confirming claims that Solange was defending the honor of her elder sister. (Of course, this is no justification for violence.)

Beyoncé articulated the agony of a generation of Black women who have had to love Black men who have been harmed and traumatized by Reaganomics, the prison industrial complex, and the drug war.

These social assaults on Black life have personal ramifications. They alter the otherwise affectionate nature of guys who come home to sleep next to you in bed. However, for the last few decades, Black women have been pathologized as the source of these issues. We've been dubbed "loud," "difficult," and "emasculating." We've been blamed for making it difficult to find loving relationships with Black guys. We have been subjected to widespread cultural gaslighting. That is, we have been labeled as insane and delusional for highlighting Black men's maltreatment of us.

When Jay-Z agreed to do what Beyoncé claimed he did, he confirmed that she was neither insane or delusional. His admission is significant. It is important that he owns it. Black women have borne a disproportionate share of the burden and responsibility for the difficulties that Black people confront in relationships. And we've had to put up with 40 years of furious Black males in hip hop telling us it's all our fault. Jay-Z is a crucial corrective to this narrative, and he opens the way for a different type of cultural conversation to take place. This cultural dialogue encourages Black male sensitivity, compassion, and empathy. This discussion is also essential because of what Black males owe to Black women. Hip hop owes Black males the opportunity to be more sophisticated and complicated characters than the clichés of ferocity and insensitivity that they frequently become in mainstream culture.

Before being fully awake, Jay reminded Harry Belafonte, who had chastised him for failing to be more political, that "his presence was charity." Thank the goddess, he's toned down some of his arrogance. His presence is not a gift, and his apologies have not helped us, but his vulnerability and courage are. I hope we can all figure out how to make good use of it.

CHAPTER 4
All Her Single Ladies

I was a teenager in Miami when Beyoncé's "Single Ladies" video debuted. I had been bullied a lot, with people calling me gay slurs before I even knew what they were or what it meant to be gay, so I spent a lot of time at home in a bubble. I'd go into my bedroom and close the door.

I was most likely viewing the "Single Ladies" video in my bedroom. When I initially saw it, I instantly began rehearsing the dancing steps. Because when I saw that, I thought to myself, "I know the girls are the gays." The gays perform these dances all the time, so they'll do this one as well. So I reasoned, "There's no way I'm going to a club or a party now and not know this dance." I must have viewed the video a million times.

My room was quite small. I didn't have much room to stand or move about. There was a big bed and a lot of furniture in my grandmother's room because it was her room before it was mine. So there wasn't much room to dance, but I made it work despite falling over a few times. I knew every step by the time I went to my next homosexual party. When "Single Ladies" came on, like I expected, I tore it up and received numerous accolades. The girls stated I was the best dancer they'd ever seen.

I'm not sure how many artists realize or accept it, but when no one else will support you, the LGBT community will. Many people are currently performing and traveling as a result of their LGBT followers. Some musicians are now waiting for Pride to arrive so they may be booked. We will stand by you even when everyone else has given up on you. That is obviously not Beyoncé, but it is important to me that musicians like her recognize our community and what we do for them.

When the video for "Single Ladies" was released, gay Black and Latino males were seen J-setting in clubs and at parties. That's the kind of dance Beyoncé was performing in the video. J-setting was going on in the bleachers behind her at Coachella lately. That enhances my bond with her because, until she did it, I had only seen homosexual guys do that type of dance. For the world's biggest performing artist to use your phrases, dance moves, and dancers is a way of indicating you deliver something worthy of recognition in the world of art and performance. It's a gigantic bear hug. I remember being in my grandmother's family room with my cousins, Crystal and Janelle, when "Bills, Bills, Bills" came out, and I remember the hair salon scene with the females talking about how bad boys were and how they weren't deserving of anything. It was instantly relatable to me—I could feel it in my spirit. I knew then that I wanted to be like Beyoncé.

By the time I graduated from high school, I had discovered Crunk & Disorderly, Concrete Loop, and other Black blogs that were both informative and hilarious. I decided to start my own. I called it Fury, and it was simply me being cynical and sassy while reporting on pop culture and strange stuff going on in everyone's backyard. That eventually led to me launching my own YouTube channel where I talked about celebrities. I'm not sure when I first mentioned Beyoncé on my channel, but the longest video I created was after a concert in Atlantic City. It was my first time seeing her live, and it certainly changed my life. I immediately returned to my hotel to tape and discuss everything that was so fantastic about her. That episode had a positive response, and I've made a video about her whenever she releases a new album or video. I speak honestly and passionately about how beautiful and otherworldly I believe she is.

Beyoncé is well aware that she has many types of admirers. Even within the Black community, she is aware that she has Southern admirers, as well as fans from the north, east, and west coasts. She is aware that she has Caribbean fans. She is aware that she has LGBT fans. I can think of times when she has included items in her artwork for each of those persons. Being of Jamaican origin, watching her sing "Sister Nancy" at Coachella made me want to cry my eyes out because I was like, What? I couldn't have asked for anything better. It's come full circle.

I've heard Beyoncé say that when she gets onstage as Sasha Fierce it's almost like she blacks out and she's a totally different person. And she doesn't even remember, half of the time, bits and pieces of the concert because there's just something else that takes over. For me, it's the same when I go onstage to do stand up, although I don't have to remember two hours of choreography and make sure I hit notes and do all of the other things she does. But even on some of the darkest days where I'm just feeling like absolute garbage, if you put a microphone in my hand and sit me onstage, I become somebody else. I give myself to my job and to the experience and I allow it to happen. That's Kid Fury.

The things I love and admire the most about Beyoncé are her work ethic and her determination and success in topping herself all the time. I always wonder, what is she going to do next? How is she going to do something bigger than this or better than this or even just as great? And she always does. Coachella reminded me about one of those aspects that I love about her so much, especially over the past few years, and that is that she has been so blatant and rich in her representation of Blackness. Her Coachella performance was the HBCU experience. She sang the national anthem, she sang "Sister Nancy" like, I'm going to take it to the Caribbean real quick. She recognizes not just her Blackness but the importance of being an artist of her stature that is celebrated by people across all racial backgrounds, ethnicities, genders, and sexualities.

She makes huge statements in her art. It's not always political. Sometimes it's doing a step routine while screaming "suck on my balls" and then twerking. That's plenty Black enough for us. But she's responsible too. She's responsible in the way that she handles her expression and her platform and her art. Nobody walks across the stage like her. Nobody commands a performance like her. Nobody swings their hair around or drops it low like she does. Beyoncé has so many dance numbers. I'm still trying to get the whole Coachella one down. My knees aren't as good as they used to be so I can't get super, super low. But I'm working on it. She has three kids and you would expect by this time she might consider giving up a little bit. That's what you love about her. She will do it pregnant, not pregnant, sick, not sick. She's going to give you a show. Because of that I will always try to keep up with the dances, but I think that "Single Ladies" is the one full routine that I will always know by heart.

CHAPTER 5
The Elevator

I've always been a peacemaker. I have a conciliatory personality that finds it difficult to comprehend any hint of aggressiveness. According to Mama, I "wouldn't say'shit' if I had a mouth full of it." Unfortunately, when someone comes for me, my first reaction is a mix of intellect and empathy—rejoinders, it appears, work on a two-hour delay. Until … The escalator. There was a moment in that oft-played video—around the 42-second mark, if you must know—that cemented Beyoncé Knowles-Carter and my unbreakable bond. Curious celebrity watchers saw a slew of things all at once: Of course, as Bey subsequently observed, "sometimes shit goes down" as it is likely to do "when it's a billion dollars in an elevator."

Jay-Z was seen repelling blow after strike. And, perhaps, we saw the basis for their upcoming "Apesh*t" video choreography. But here's the truth. That was a very intimate time for The Queen and me. We were connected as she gazed, not with reverence, but with pleasure, at her man's pain. Bey became real to me at the 42-second mark. That's exactly right. I no longer saw a cultural icon, a flawlessly curved caramel-colored ideal vision of feminine form. I didn't even see the nearly snatched margins framing poreless skin and the 220-gram honey-blonde dipped extensions. I honestly believe I saw right into her soul. My heart wasn't just stitched into Beyoncé's; I was Beyoncé—sorta, kinda, with a short cut, a smallish butt, and a B-cup. She'd definitely been concealing secrets, just like me. Bey, who hid behind a sweet-smiled curtain of respectability, was just as angry and lonely as I was.

Beyoncé is a phenomenally talented international megastar. She physically embodies our cultural beauty standards, or comes as close as most human beings can. She is extremely affluent. Millions of people adore her. Since the late '90s, she has held America's celebrity infatuation prisoner. But life isn't that easy. Because, at the end of the night, Bey is a Black woman who loves and is married to a Black guy. And that is a difficult task. It's a multi-layered, gorgeous, and rich item. But it's more than that because Black love is DIFFICULT.

We aspire to be The Good Wife, The Good Husband, The Nice House, and The Cute Kids. We want to appear to be doing The Good Job, maintaining The Tight Body, and rocking The Right 'Do. It's a lot of labor, but we do it with our mouths turned up almost reflexively.

Until ... The Elevator. Solange Knowles beat Jay-Z like he stole something, deftly wielding her copper-colored $1,600 evening purse in a tiny crook of the 35-square-foot cab. Lil's is smacked, kicked, and scratched Jigga in a ferocious display of whoop ass. As impressed as we were by Solange's WWE prowess, none of her moves could compete with Queen Bey's immobile stance. A keen observer, such as myself, noticed that Beyoncé did not raise an eyebrow in support of her husband. Instead, she stood in silent support of his whipping, dressed nicely in Givenchy couture and sporting a painted-on smile. She wanted him to suffer for as long as she had. It was both shocking and strangely familiar to watch.

The loop of TMZ's three-minute video footage resonated through the nation's collective mind to astonishing effect that day in May 2014. Since the two met in or around 1999... or 2000, depending on which celebrity magazine you read, the Carter-Knowles relationship has been shrouded in secrecy. In a maddened celebrity society so prevalent that the public is informed on intimacies like Gwyneth Paltrow's vagina steams, Gabrielle Union's preference for booty-licking sex, and everything in between, their shrouded marital relationships speak volumes. Oprah even exposes her secrets. Details of the Carter-Knowles marriage, on the other hand, are as tightly guarded as the al-Qaeda fortress of Tora Bora.

Solange got in bruh-man's face after the first few Beckys and said, through clenched teeth and cut-eye glances, "Look here..." She spoke for a long time, emphasizing his mistakes and the impending repercussions. And, as I heard my sister say several times, Solange closed with the words: "Mofo, trust and believe!" You have one more chance..." Hence ... The Elevator. Clearly, previous attempts had failed, leaving Solange with no choice. She went completely insane. That footage sent me back to the playground, when I witnessed my sister bodyslam a pitiful soul on my behalf. When you have a sis like mine and Bey's, you don't divulge every slight from a culprit to them. Call it a gut feeling, sibling intuition, or mercy. But, as the peaceful sibling, I know that my brawling sister will not give me as many do-overs as I will.

When Jay released a follow-up—admitting his transgressions on I Gave You Lemons—the internet went Lemonade wild, and the world virtually bowed at his feet.

And I knew from her thin smile that Bey had been putting on a brave face for many, many years. Because being the "nice" sister implies that your entire existence should be, well... lovely. And when you are the "peacemaker"—even if only in your own mind—you naturally don't want to disturb the peace of everyone's view. That would be a disaster. It would make a commotion. Keep your cool. If you have a husband who appears to do everything a husband should do. A husband who appears to be the part, exudes charm, and isn't "nearly as bad as a lot of men out there." Simply smile and suffer it. Things might go much worse.

Of course, this is just supposition on my part. Bey's expression is typical of a perfect woman. I mean, I may or may not be a people pleaser. But I know what it's like to do and not do some things in a take-one-for-the-team show of support. The first time becomes the third, then the seventeenth, and finally a full-fledged habit. After all, our brothers have a lot on their plates. Black women are taught that life is easier for them. We are capable of handling more. Be courteous. Smile. Act as if everything is fine. Determine how to make him shine. Deny yourself all of the parts of yourself that you worked so hard to create. Be lovely. Don't forget to be pleasant. And delectable.

To be clear, I am not a Beyoncé fan. Really, I never have. I'm not sure I understand or trust the Beyhive at all. That amount of devotion worries me. Nonetheless, I appreciate and admire Beyoncé... a lot. I recall strolling through downtown Brooklyn with "No, No, No" screaming so loudly that it might as well have been my theme tune. I could hear it from every double-parked jeep on Flatbush Avenue, and even when it wasn't playing.

   I recall young Supremes with tight press-and-curls back in the days of Wyclef, Kelly Rowland, LeToya Luckett, and the other booted Child. Beyoncé seized center stage even before she filled out the form, got a weave, or engaged a stylist. Behind Beyoncé's eyes was a knowingness that seemed to magnify her superstar status. Solo Bey was not a "if" but rather a "when." I know it sounds corny. But it was as if she sensed her fate. Until … The Elevator. Seeing her stand witness to her husband's beating reminded me of the inner-knowingness that pulled me in the first place. Beyoncé was put in the elevator, but she wasn't there; she was somewhere else. Only this time her eyes revealed a less-than-ideal future.

Where there had been optimism, there was despair and emptiness. The blank in her stare also reminded me that, up until that videotaped scuffle, I hadn't been experiencing Bey for over a decade. We hadn't exactly fought. She was more like that excellent girlfriend you used to hang out with but had lost contact with—who you hadn't seen or heard from in months. Beyoncé influenced me years before she was crazy in love, and later drunk in love.

She kept me entertained over time with smart dance numbers like "Get Me Bodied" and "Freakum Dress." Beyoncé has unquestionably earned her legendary position as a performer and musical artist. She began to change her tune in the time it took to fold her Dereon pants. And by the time she got to "Bow Down," in early 2013, I was completely fed up. I didn't mind a confident Beyoncé announcing her dominance... all facts. But what was she so enraged about? And to what gang of babes, was Bey's rage directed? The juxtaposition of a rage-fueled tirade against haters with a snippet of Chimamanda Ngozi Adichie's "We Should All Be Feminists" didn't help matters:

We teach girls to shrink themselves ... Otherwise, you would threaten the man ... marriage can be a source of joy and love and mutual support but why do we teach girls to aspire to marriage and we don't teach boys the same?

To finish the song, we hear Beyoncé's aggressive posturing (God damn, God damn!) about waking up like this and how her guy made her feel so God damn fine.

I think males are beautiful, but I don't believe women should attribute everything they do to men: "Did he hurt me, do I forgive him, did he put a ring on my finger?" Don't misunderstand me. I'm also a walking contradiction. And I'm all for the complexities of an artist. Bey is bold to move in her creativity, in my opinion. The paradoxes that both feed and torture creatives are part of what distinguishes them from the rest of the world.

We are both brilliant and naive, cocky but insecure, playful and disciplined, extroverted and introverted in equal measure. However, intellectualizing her multidimensional demeanor could not compensate for the reality that Bey was beginning to wear on me. For a while, I had the impression she was on the point of overexposure. Remember when she appeared to be on TV as much as the NBC peacock? Every awards ceremony. Remember when she felt the need to bogart the 2015 Grammys, knowing full well that the vastly underrated Ledisi should've had a Selma "Precious Lord" moment? It's strange how Bey, the Oshun goddess, reclaimed the Holy Spirit once 25 million viewers were at stake. That was disgusting. It wasn't an unforgivable offense, just a strange one. Who was she, really?

I can't talk from personal experience with cultural icons. But, in my opinion, there must come a period when you no longer need to prove to the world how attractive or provocative you are. Bey, we see you. We've been keeping an eye out for you. So, what are you doing out here the most? I was furious. Until … The escalator. That 3:32 video loop explained everything. What it revealed was a Black woman who was just as broken, strong, bewildered, certain, hungry, wise, lacking, complete, proud, and vulnerable as I was. I admire her for it.

CHAPTER 6
The Art of Being Beyoncé

She is huddled, surrounded by white, pink, burgundy, and yellow poppies, peonies, orchids, and roses. She's staring at the camera with no sign of nervousness in her eyes. She is semi-naked, veiled, with a prominently bulging belly. On February 1, 2017, Beyoncé Knowles-Carter announced to the world via her Instagram account that she is expecting twins. We can't take our eyes off everything in the photograph because it's so artistic and tempting. A few hours later, other images from the same series begin to appear on her website and subsequently spread over the internet.

Everyone rushes to deconstruct and decipher every image, creating an instant media frenzy. According to New York University art historian Dennis Geronimus, the green veil is an homage to Our Lady of Guadalupe, the patroness of the Mexican Catholic Church. Adrianna Campbell, an art historian, sees connections to the work of Mexican artist Frida Kahlo. The connections to Venus, the Roman goddess of sex, love, and fertility, are particularly strong in these works, relating directly to Sandro Botticelli's fifteenth-century masterpiece "The Birth of Venus." In one of the photos, Beyoncé is naked on a pedestal surrounded by beautiful tropical flora, concealing a breast with one hand and embracing her belly with the other, her cascading hair wrapping around the side of her body. In another, in black and white, she sits on a flower throne, her countenance more demure, almost virginal. If it weren't for her enlarged midriff.

At the end of 2009, I was around seven months pregnant with my youngest son. I went to Tracy Anderson's exercise studio in New York City (then in a loft on Hubert Street) one morning in December. Beyoncé arrived by my side as I was about to begin my daily workout. More impressively, she noticed me. When I told my husband later that day, he remarked, "And how could she not?" Needless to say, I stood out in a 90-degree heated room, dancing and contorting in tight exercise clothes and a massive tummy. "B" stared at me and my tummy with grace, astonishment, excitement, and a wide, warm Southern smile, dressed in black leggings and a gray tank top, hair up in a ponytail, bare-faced, taller and much more lovely than in all her images and movies. "Congratulations!" she said, and we shared a little moment of sisterhood.

That day, it dawned on me that Beyoncé's artistry is as much about empathy, sensitivity, and compassion as it is about inventiveness, all of which are necessary qualities for a great and lasting artist. Our contemporary art sometimes refers to the past, sometimes seeks to reveal the future, but largely it allows us to evaluate the present, and on many occasions, it holds up a mirror in which we may see ourselves.

Beyoncé, an art collector herself, told The New York Times in a profile about her mother, Tina Lawson, that growing up: "it was important to my mother to surround us with positive, powerful, strong images of African and African American art so that we could reflect and see ourselves in them … My mother has always been invested in making women feel beautiful, and her art collection always told the stories of women wanting to do the same."

It's hardly surprising, then, that Beyoncé is still fascinated by art and makes references to it whenever she has a relevant opportunity. Music, dance, film, visual arts, and performance all have something in common: they make life more fascinating. All of these artistic representations, either together or separately, broaden our souls, expand our spirits, and provide us with new perspectives.

Beyoncé incorporates all of them: in songs, visuals, concerts, and films that urge reflection on the African diaspora, what it means to be a Black woman in America, or simply what it means to be a woman in today's society. The ultimate goal of self-expression is an insatiable need to bridge the gap between us. The gap that divides us as humans, that feeling that we all have at some point in our lives that makes us feel misunderstood or alone, can only be bridged by our shared universal experiences: grief, shame, sexual instinct, joy, sadness, ecstasy, sorrow, fear, euphoria, and love.

Beyoncé is a master of such quotations. Consider the video for "Mine," which was released as part of her eponymous album in 2013. Beyoncé goes slowly, the lighting is pure and clean, and she is dressed in a heavy veil and a strapless gown that has the appearance of marble, like the surface of a sculpture. A male model sits on her lap. It is a direct homage to Michelangelo Buonarroti's "La Pieta," a 1499 Carrara marble Renaissance sculpture regarded as one of the greatest works by one of the greatest artists of all time. Later in the film, a guy and a woman kiss while their heads are clothed in white. They appear to be inspired by Belgian surrealist René Magritte's picture "The Lovers." Beyoncé blends Italian Renaissance, surrealism, R&B, and African sounds with ease. Consider modern-day syncretism.

In "Hold Up," at the intersection of art, music, fashion, and performance, Beyoncé draws inspiration from Swiss artist Pipilotti Rist's 1997 double screen "Ever Is Over All," which debuted at that year's Venice Biennale. A Google search of her name will get the word "Beyoncé" in third place, indicating that people want to know how contemporary art has impacted Beyoncé, and in the process, they have learnt about numerous artists, Rist being just one of them.) Rist's piece depicts the artist walking down the street in a turquoise dress and red heels, smashing the windows of parked automobiles with a gigantic flower in a graceful and feminine manner. In "Hold Up," Beyoncé is dressed in a flowing, sensual amber organza dress and black platforms. She swings a baseball bat with fire on her hips and her trademark swagger, smashing car windows, store vitrines, hydrants, and video cameras. It's a conundrum for both Rist and Beyoncé: fragile beings engaging in aggressive behavior while smiling broadly.

Beyoncé's favorite visual genre is likewise Afro-Futurism. In the video for "Sorry," Nigerian artist Laolu Senbanjo painted geometric shapes on the dancers' bodies. He titled his paintings the Sacred Art of the Ori, referring to a spiritual Yoruba rite. Keith Haring's art and the way he painted on vocalist Grace Jones's body for her live performance at New York City's Paradise Garage in 1985 have striking parallels. Beyoncé's performance at the Grammy Awards in February 2017, shortly after announcing her second pregnancy, was also laced with Afro-Futuristic influences. We picture her clothed as a goddess, as if she is redeeming the entire Black race by casting a light into the world.

Her gown was designed by Peter Dundas and was inspired by Gustav Klimt's golden period, with ornate Art Deco patterns inspired by Erté. Although Byzantine in construction and aesthetics, the gilded halo is an homage to Oshun, whose symbolism abounds in Beyoncé's videos and performances. The colors associated with the Yoruba goddess of fecundity, sexuality, beauty, love, luxury, and pleasure are yellow, gold, and amber, all of which she loves and prominently displays with her fertile body. Beyoncé and Jay-Z stunned the world when they released Everything Is Love in the summer of 2018. The first promotional track, "Apesh*t," had its music video shot at the Louvre in Paris. The Carters and their dancers move through the museum's regal galleries, creating contrast and tension between their own bodies as contemporary pop icons and artworks such as the Mona Lisa, Venus de Milo, and the Winged Victory of Samothrace, all identifiable historical treasures that have withstood the test of time without losing their allure. I'm particularly taken with the scene in which Beyoncé appears with her troupe of dancers, all of whom are women of varied body types, all of whom are Black, and all of whom are dressed in flesh-toned leotards, leggings, and short tops.

They stare defiantly at the camera beneath the massive painting, "The Consecration of the Emperor Napoleon I and Coronation of the Empress Josephine in the Cathedral of Notre-Dame de Paris on 2 December 1804," by the preeminent French Neoclassical painter Jacques-Louis David, completed in 1807 after being commissioned directly by Napoleon Bonaparte. The picture represents Napoleon's coronation as Emperor of France, as well as the coronation of his wife Josephine, in front of Notre Dame's altar and a vast assemblage of dignitaries, including Pope Pius VII. What I find interesting, if not subversive, is that historians depicted Napoleon as a sexist who did not regard women as equal to males and referred to them as "nothing but machines for producing children." The contrast between Napoleon and everything he represented and Beyoncé's feminist, open-minded, egalitarian, and democratic mindset makes the scene at the Louvre seem and feel like an electric shock to history.

In considering her contributions to art and entertainment, pop culture, and the world at large, I've come to feel that Beyoncé has found a way to redefine the power of the image by fusing classic and contemporary, western and non-western, divine and profane. She has established her own language in order to honor and elevate African Americans, women, and free expression. It is acceptable and even desirable to be sexual, curvy, to be a muse to many and a muse to oneself, to love our bodies, to love our husbands, to be devoted mothers, and, in Beyoncé's case, to insert herself into the most iconic works of art in ways that no other performer has ever done. She is a creator whose imprint on our culture has earned her a place in art history.

CHAPTER 7
Grown Women: A Conversation with an Icon About Coming of Age

When the sun refuses to rise, even after midday. When my inner Sasha is unable to locate the zip code of fierce—that's when I reach for the white cup with a dishwasher-faded gray message: I'm suffering from a bad case of not being Beyoncé. This was not always the case. It's strange that she's become my barometer. Even Destiny's Child didn't appeal to me. There is no shade. However, I am twelve years her senior. Little Beyoncé and her pals—"Wait, isn't one of them her sister?" "Girl, I don't know, turn up that En Vogue!" didn't do it for me. Then 2003. I had matured. Married. The new mother of a baby girl. Beyoncé had gone "crazy in love."

I was in the living room the first time I saw the footage. My graduate student was cooking. "Dani!" I yelled at her. Come on in. Take a look at this! Beyoncé got some, and it was clearly mutual. And it was unquestionably good." We went back and watched it again. We got it memorized for the third time. Dani is no longer my graduate student after fifteen years. She is a colleague on my faculty. But if the DJ plays "Crazy in Love," we clear the dance floor with a time-tested routine. It's difficult to acknowledge as a feminist academic, a political scientist, and a participant in LGBT movements, but it was the sex that drew me in. This girl-to-woman transition was immediately recognized. It brought back memories of the first time I felt wanted and satisfied by sex. I grinned like a proud big sister as I watched Beyoncé's crazy love unfold.

I was engrossed in Beyoncé's journey. She wasn't me, but the niece, daughter, or student. Younger. Prettier. Far more talented, but linked, so that youth, beauty, and talent inspire pride rather than competition. The plural form of the first person. We. As an aunt, mother, and educator. From here, I can read her calmly, even joyfully.

MANKAPRR CONTEH

When the sun does not rise after midday. When my inner Sasha can't find the ferocious zip code, I grab for the white cup with a dishwasher-faded gray message: I'm suffering from a horrible case of not being Beyoncé. This was not always true. It's odd that she's become my yardstick. I didn't even like Destiny's Child. There is no cover. I am, however, twelve years her senior. "Wait, isn't one of them her sister?" says little Beyoncé. "Girl, I don't know, turn up that En Vogue!" just didn't do it for me. Then 2003. I'd grown up. Married. A new mother with a baby girl. Beyoncé was "crazy in love."

The first time I viewed the footage, I was in the living room. My graduate student was in the kitchen. "Dani!" I screamed at her. Please come in. Examine this out! Beyoncé got some, and it was obvious that it was reciprocal. And it was undeniably excellent." We returned to see it again. By the third time, we had it memorized. Dani has graduated from my graduate program after fifteen years. She is one of my colleagues on the faculty. But if the DJ plays "Crazy in Love," we have a tried-and-true procedure for clearing the dance floor. It's difficult to admit as a feminist professor, political scientist, and LGBT activist, but it was the sex that drew me in. This shift from girl to lady was immediately recognized. It reminded me of the first time I felt wanted and gratified by sex. As I watched Beyoncé's love life unfold, I grinned like a proud big sister.

I was completely engaged in Beyoncé's journey. She wasn't me, but someone else's niece, daughter, or pupil. Younger. Prettier. Far more gifted, but linked in such a way that youth, attractiveness, and talent inspire pride rather than competition. The first person plural form.

We. As an aunt, a mother, and a teacher. I can read her calmly, even gleefully, from here.

MANKAPRR CONTEH

When Beyoncé stops the world, I am a sophomore at Wake Forest University working on the fame-for-good thing. I think about death far too frequently. My silver Corolla has been replaced by a sleek black Honda Civic that I see careening over an overpass. Beyoncé has the audacity to create an exceptional self-titled hip-hop-n-b visual album on which she publicly admits that she struggles with being beautiful. She is so committed to this confession that she makes "Pretty Hurts" the first tune on the album and a single. I'm both cute and sad, yet the two have absolutely nothing to do with one other.

I'm rushing away from the school that ignited a dormant and clinical depression, fleeing north for one month of wintry freedom. This album makes me feel free. It jolts my tired muscles and my sluggish pulse. I'm texting people about how fantastic the music is, and I'm giving up the driver's seat. I think her self-titled album is a musical masterpiece, but I see flaws in "Bow Down," "***Flawless," and the album as a whole as feminist manifestos, according to Melissa Harris-Perry. If Beyoncé adores women so much, why is she acting so crazy around us? Who are these ladies she's urging to kneel, and what have they done to avoid Beyoncé's feminism?

I've joined a Black sorority, I'm dating a pro-Black nationally ranked debater, and I've started thinking a lot about womanhood and race—so much so that I've decided to plan and co-organize a forum on "feminism and race in the age of Beyoncé" in the spring. I ask a classroom of colleagues how they feel about their own feminist sensibilities, Miley Cyrus's twerking, Olivia Pope's commandeering, and Beyoncé's career, and how and why we understand all of them the way we do. When we are advised to enter "Formation," I am returning to university for a second semester after a one-year sabbatical. The previous year, it was like leave or die, so I did. Melissa Harris-Perry will be a Wake Forest faculty member when I return. I'm pleased I moved away to try to get my life in order the same year she arrived on campus. I wish I could be her. I'm taking her course on the history of Black liberation movements, which is called after the current one: Black Lives Matter.

It's the first class held since Beyoncé marched into Levi's Stadium with a Black power militia of gyrating dancers. It's the first class since Beyoncé launched her first single and music video in two years like an anthemic bomb. Beyoncé rejects racial ambiguity in this video. Knowing and loving Beyoncé, she says, means knowing and loving her man's negro nose, her baby's afro, her Southern heritage, and her disgust with state-sanctioned Black death. But here's Beyoncé, acting as if hard work is the key to success, I think and tell Prof. MHP. Here's Beyoncé, pushing us to go for the night unreachable heights of capitalism rather than breaking down its oppressive barriers. Here is Beyoncé, selling "Formation" merchandise that is likely expensive for the communities seen in the film and likely created by impoverished people all over the world, as I suppose her Ivy Park line is. And, while I believe Beyoncé is concerned about state brutality against Black people and wants the cops to stop killing us, I can't remove the idea that she waited to say so until it was popular—when it was safe for her image and her coffers. "Formation" strikes me as taking a relatively center-left stance, despite the fact that its performer possesses the social and material wherewithal to go further.

HARRIS-PERRY, MELISSA

I summoned my beloved student in 2003 to observe Beyoncé's development. Dani and I have been dancing since then. For more than a decade, I encouraged readers and viewers to watch, study, celebrate, and enjoy King Beyoncé's skill. Everyone showed up. I went to the potluck. I delivered plates to the table. Feasted on her majesty. All these years later, I'd called my students back to the table, but only one would come. Mankaprr pushed back, a little disgusted but primarily uninterested. A vegan for life offers steak and potatoes. "I suppose I can see why other people might find it nourishing, but it does nothing for me."

THE MANKAPRR CONTEH

I'm overjoyed right before we tried the Lemonade. I am filled with purpose, hope, excitement, and brightness. Dr. Harris-Perry's Anna Julia Cooper Center for Intersectional Scholarship employs me as a communications intern. I've been escorted to Debra Lee's home for the BET Honors. I've sparred with Arsenio Hall, taken selfies with Eric Holder, and spoken with a Washington Post reporter. I'm delighted I kept my Honda Civic running. The following day, Dr. Harris-Perry requests that we write. She's putting together a Lemonade roundtable for ELLE.com and wants Camry and me to participate. It is my first chance to get published in a national outlet—in any outlet other than my high school newspaper. We stayed up all night in the basement of Wake Forest's soaring business school, hooking up our laptop to a projector and listening to Lemonade via Prof. MHP's husband's Tidal account. And I see my life, my objectives, and myself in Beyoncé's art for the first time.

MELISSA HARRIS-PERRY

2016 was the most difficult year of my adult life. The bitterness of what had been consumed lingered in my mouth like the sour metal of an enslaved bit. There is so much to say. I am yelling. However, no one can hear me any longer. At my own funeral, people treat me as if I were a ghost. I moved closer to the edge. Unwilling to use the fading mug on a daily basis. Then Beyoncé and Mankaprr began collaborating on projects. Bey drank Lemonade while folding time. I preferred the position of teacher over the one of pupil. Bey and I stood on the cliff together. How could she have known that in my gloom, I was always wondering what it would be like to jump? How long would it take for the snow to fall? Will it hurt if I fall to the ground? Beyoncé took my hand in hers. I was shown. The plural form of the first person. We took a leap of faith. Instead, we tumbled into the sea. Beyoncé turned the classroom upside down. I assumed Socratic authorship. The inquiries were coerced. What if we put Black girls' and women's hopes, dreams, sorrow, joy, loss, bodies, voices, stories, expressions, styles, families, history, and futures in the center and started from there?

MANKAPRR CONTEH

Beyoncé's agony may not seem like mine, with self-loathing, guilt, and crippling fear. As Professor Blair L. M. Kelley points out, it appears to be sadness, bitterness, and the strong bedrock of Christian monogamy being ripped from beneath her. She let us all witness her pain. Beyoncé seems to want me to know in Lemonade that she knows my latent hatred, that it makes sense, that it is genuine, that beauty may hurt her, but it also helps her so much. No other image captures the tragic truth of that statement better. "The violence of African colonialism, the enslavement of West Africans, the dehumanization of their ancestors in Katrina, and our continued erasure through capitalism and gentrification—all depicted in mere seconds," I contribute to the roundtable discussion. To think Beyoncé did all of this in an album perhaps inspired by her husband's transgressions; to think she extended her sorrow to generations of strife; and to think she lent her power to all of us, to women of every shade, class, and Blackness, is to think about Beyoncé in ways I never thought I would.

MELISSA HARRIS-PERRY

I've made this error before. I assumed the split was generational. Or perhaps regional. Or it could be socioeconomic. When I was blinded by my own lofty golden privilege all along. Let me count the number of times my BFF has gotten me into "Formation" about this particular redbone craze. I keep missing the genius Mankaprr's brown girl agony. I miss it and notice it. Mankaprr, too, wants to jump. I pray the prayers that you are not permitted to pray. I close transactions. I want all the sour. Keep the sweet for her. But I'm not like Bey. Yellow lemon. When we mean to comfort, we sting. I keep forgetting about it. Even when Beyoncé got closer and closer to nailing it. So it was Mankaprr, not me, who sent the invitation to the table when the pomp and circumstance, Divine 9 repping, Drum Major high dancing, and Lifting Every Voice to Sing burst forth across Beychella. In the middle of the night, I received a message. "MHP, please tell me you are watching this."

"When Everything Is Love."

MANKAPRR CONTEH

With the enthusiasm of late afternoon, I watch Beychella in the early hours of the morning. As Bey transforms the main stage of the country's most infamous music festival into an HBCU homecoming, I cheer and hug my lover Neicy. I'm so moved and entertained that I cry. I'm joining the ranks of people of all genders who recognize she's just done something monumental. When I think of how I swayed and twerked and complained and cried to her performance, what it felt like to revel in unbound joy, I can't help but think it was liberation. And I can't help but think Beyoncé wants Black folks to realize that liberation is possible if we keep dreaming."

MELISSA HARRIS-PERRY

Mankaprr has been won by Beyoncé. She has won her over with brown girl dreams of loving her people, remembering her past, looking forward to the future, dancing with her sister, and singing with her guy. Mankaprr, the lone child of African immigrant parents, has been won over by Bey's ambition of a brown female college for her new offspring. Then there will be a scholarship fund. Without a doubt. I went over the text. Organize a Lemonade roundtable. Invite everyone to write. But, in reality, it was not called by me. It's Mankaprr this time. I recently received the byline. That's when I realized my allegiance had altered. Beyhive is still my name. Lifetime platinum member. Forever. But, fifteen years after she won me over with "Crazy in Love," I watched "Apesh*t" with disdain. I smiled but was unmoved. There is no need to write. If words must be penned, they will come from Mankaprr.

MANKAPRR CONTEH

I still watch "Apesh*t" and wonder what it may have meant and done for Black culture if Beyoncé had shot it at a Black museum instead of the Louvre, but I understand why she did it. I understand why she wanted to express that we are more lovely and valuable than anything else in there. I wonder what it would have meant for Beyoncé to make protest music after the deaths of Amadou Diallo, Sean Bell, Oscar Grant, or Aiyana Stanley-Jones; but I understand that she, like many of us—including myself—didn't become truly outraged until George Zimmerman was found not guilty of Trayvon Martin's murder. I consider the $1.5 million she and Jay-Z have donated to the Black Lives Matter movement. In Lemonade, she included Sybrina Fulton, Lezley McSpadden, and Gwen Carr in all their regality and misery. But I understand. That's where I stand with Beyoncé. I finally understand. I understand that she operates under the constraints of capitalism; I also understand that she did not join up to demolish them. I understand that she wants her children's children's children to be extremely well off; I understand that she undoubtedly wants this as much as she wants freedom for all of us. I understand what she means to many Black women, including ladies I adore. I understand what she represents to many Black folks. I understand what she means to me. I still don't want to be a pop star, but I recognize that Beyoncé is recognized for something positive.

MELISSA HARRIS-PERRY

Beyoncé's gift exceeds my expectations. She bound me to the journey, not to herself. Invested in my ability. The performance. The world's creation. Bey creates the universe. It was fantastic. Mankaprr unmade and recreated it. This is what brown females fantasize about: In her 2014 memoir Brown Girl Dreaming, Jacqueline Woodson describes it.

CHAPTER 8
What Queen Bey Means to Everyone

The Definitive Beyoncé Biography

ACCORDING TO WIKIPEDIA

In my memories, most of my personal accomplishments have a Beyoncé song as the soundtrack. I couldn't stop listening to "Crazy in Love" while planning my wedding. When I became a mother, "Single Ladies (Put a Ring on It)" was a smash hit with the toddler set, including my son. He and I laughed as we attempted and failed to dance like Beyoncé in the song, watching instructional videos on how to imitate her moves. That was one of the first occasions he and I established a common interest. I wondered what data analysis may show about what Beyoncé means to other people as I considered how she has been a constant presence in my own life. (As a data journalist, I'm constantly curious about how to measure things.)

I started with Wikipedia. The Wikipedia biography of Beyoncé is like a glimpse into the collective psyche of how other people perceive Beyoncé. Beyonce's life is divided into eras based on her albums, according to Wikipedia. Reading about her achievements, it's evident that each stage of her career has brought her exponentially greater success—and that she has been in control of the entire process. Her career management is an inspiration to me as I consider what I want my own life to be like in the future.

1997–2001: DESTINY'S CHILD

FEB 1998
Destiny's Child released its self-titled debut album.
JUL 1999

Destiny's Child released its second studio album, The Writing's on the Wall, which Billboard has ranked #39 in its Top 200 Albums of the Decade.
FEB 2001
Beyoncé won her first Grammy with Destiny's Child for "Say My Name" at the 43rd Annual Grammy Awards.
MAY 2001
Destiny's Child released Survivor, which debuted at #1 on the U.S. Billboard 200.
OCT 2001
Destiny's Child went on hiatus.

2002–2005: DANGEROUSLY IN LOVE
JUL 2002
Beyoncé starred as Foxxy Cleopatra alongside Mike Myers in the hit movie Austin Powers in Goldmember, showing the world that she can act as well as sing and dance like a dream.
JUN 2003
Dangerously in Love, Beyoncé's first solo album, launched. The album's lead single, "Crazy in Love," featuring Jay-Z, became Beyoncé's first #1 single as a solo artist in the United States.
FEB 2004
On February 1, Beyoncé performed the American national anthem at Super Bowl XXXVIII in her hometown of Houston, Texas. A week later, she earned five awards at the 46th Annual Grammy Awards, putting her well on her way to becoming one of the most-decorated recording artists of all time.
NOV 2004
Destiny's Child fulfilled its destiny by releasing its final studio album, Destiny Fulfilled.
DEC 2005
Beyoncé was nominated for a Golden Globe award for her role in Dreamgirls alongside Jennifer Hudson, Jamie Foxx, and Eddie Murphy.

2006–2007: B'DAY

SEPT 2006

Beyoncé released her second solo album, B'Day, on her twenty-fifth birthday.

2008–2010: I AM ... SASHA FIERCE

APR 2008

On 4/4, Beyoncé married Jay-Z.

OCT 2008

I Am ... Sasha Fierce dropped on November 18, with the listening party on October 22. Beyoncé shot the video for its monster hit song "Single Ladies (Put a Ring on It)" on what was a scorching hot day **in New York City, in a studio without air-conditioning. #hot**

JAN 2009

Beyoncé performed at President Barack Obama's first inaugural ball.

MAR 2010

Beyoncé and her mother, Tina Knowles, opened The Beyoncé Cosmetology Center at Phoenix House Career Academy in Brooklyn, a training center for women and men in treatment for drug addiction. Beyoncé also took a nine-month break from performing, her longest hiatus ever.

2011–2012: 4

JUN 2011

Beyoncé released her fourth studio album, 4.

JUL 2011

Beyoncé wrote an essay, "Eat, Play, Love," for Essence about her 2010 career break. The piece won a writing award from the New York Association of Black Journalists.

JAN 2012

Beyoncé gave birth to her first child, Blue Ivy Carter.

2013–2014: BEYONCÉ

JAN 2013

Beyoncé performed at President Obama's second inauguration in Washington, D.C.

FEB 2013

Beyoncé performed at the Super Bowl XLVII halftime show, held at the Mercedes-Benz Superdome in New Orleans. Life Is But a Dream, a feature-length documentary film about and co-directed by Beyoncé, aired on HBO.

APR 2013

The Mrs. Carter Show World Tour began on April 15. The 132-date tour began in Serbia.

DEC 2013

Beyoncé released her fifth album without warning, and straight to iTunes, much to the surprise of her fans.

APR 2014

Beyoncé and husband, Jay-Z, announced their On the Run Tour, the first time they headlined a stadium tour together.

2016–2017: LEMONADE

FEB 2016

Another surprise for fans was the availability of "Formation" on Beyoncé's music streaming platform, Tidal. The first live performance of "Formation" was at the Super Bowl L halftime show that year.

APR 2016

Lemonade, an album and a one-hour HBO film, were all released by Beyoncé. It set a new record for the most-streamed album by a female artist in one week, with fans streaming the album 115 million times on Tidal. It sold 1.554 million copies in the United States and went on to become the best-selling album of the year internationally, selling 2.5 million copies worldwide.

JUN 2017

Beyoncé gave birth to twins Rumi and Sir Carter.

SEPT 2017

Beyoncé worked with J. Balvin and Willy William to release a remix of "Mi Gente," with earnings benefiting those affected by Hurricane Harvey and Hurricane Irma in Texas, Mexico, Puerto Rico, and other Caribbean islands.

2018: EVERYTHING IS LOVE

APR 2018

Beyoncé headlined the Coachella Music Festival in April 2018. Her YouTube appearance became the most-watched live performance on the website all time.

JUN 2018

At the commencement of their On the Run II tour, Beyoncé and Jay-Z released their first joint studio album, Everything Is Love. The album was a surprise release, announced on Tidal with the message "Album out now" after they finished a London performance. The first video, for the tune "Apesh*t," was shot at the Louvre and portrays the couple standing alone with the Mona Lisa, the world's most renowned painting. Beyoncé is as much a part of our collective cultural awareness as Leonardo da Vinci.

Looking for Beyoncé

Google records everything individuals type into the Google Search box, and the Google Trends tool displays what people are looking for.1 They are frequently looking for Queen Bey. These two graphs depict Google Trends data on where and when the world turns into a Beyhive. The chart on the left lists the states of the United States in order of their interest in searching for the term "Beyoncé." The chart on the right shows when Beyoncé searches peaked. These peaks, in general, correspond to newsworthy moments in Bey's life—the same events that Wikipedians document. It's as though Beyoncé's big moments are shared by millions of people.

CHAPTER 9
Beyoncé, Influencer

Beyoncé had given birth to Blue Ivy in January 2012, thus it had been a month. There were no images, only the baby's first cries, which were recorded on Jay-Z's latest track. What might the offspring of a nice girl transformed into a ferocious musical queen and a bad boy transformed into a music mogul look like? Whom would she model herself after? What would she be wearing in her first photos as the heiress of fashion royalty? After Angelina Jolie and Brad Pitt auctioned off the first images of their baby Shiloh, the baby celebrity picture market heated up. According to People magazine, the deal totaled $4 million in 2005. The first photographs of their twins, Vivienne and Knox, topped it in 2008, with a whopping $14 million, all of which was donated to charity.

Celebrities no longer needed People or Access Hollywood to promote themselves. They immediately approached their followers via social media, where they exposed the most sensitive elements of their life. As a result, they hastened the disintermediation of the press in favor of platforms. This is not to say that Instagram and Facebook have freed Hollywood from the constraints of image control. They have, in some ways, had the opposite impact, establishing self-censorship as the standard. Any true friend will seek your permission before uploading a photo of you.

At the time of writing, Beyoncé has 118 million Instagram followers, which appears to be her preferred medium, most likely due to its extremely visual nature. Beyoncé's direct audience interaction has been critical to the success of her last three album releases, where surprise and coordination were crucial strategies. Beyoncé was the most influential social media celebrity in 2017, according to D'Marie Analytics, and her Instagram posts are worth more than $1,000,000 in advertising value each. Even if she collected endorsement fees for only a tenth of her 1,637 Instagram posts, that would translate to $100 million in advertising value. She's not just the model; she's also the medium.

It's unclear who pictures Beyoncé on a daily basis, but it's evident that every facet of her life is filmed. Jay-Z is seen shooting her in one image, and he could be the source of some of those posts. According to Refinery29: When Jay Z isn't moonlighting as a musician, he's the world's most sought-after Instagram Husband. Shawn Carter has been teasing his side hustle for years. "When I was talking Instagram The last thing you wanted was your picture snapped," he says in Magna Carta Holy Grail's "Somewhere in America."

According to GQ, Beyoncé maintains an archive of every shot ever taken of her in her workplace area. "There, across from the narrow conference room where you're interviewing her, is another long, narrow room that contains the official Beyoncé archive, a temperature-controlled digital-storage facility that contains virtually every existing photograph of her, starting with the very first frames taken of Destiny's Child, the '90s girl group she once fronted; every interview she's ever done; every video of every show she's ever performed; every diary she's ever kept," the writer wrote.

Beyoncé's first Instagram post was on November 6, 2012, the day Barack Obama won his second term as President. Her initial post (using the handle "Baddie Bey") had her wearing a T-shirt that read, "Texans for Obama." "After Obama's victory was announced, she posted a second photo of a handwritten note that read 'Take that, Mitches,' in reference to the Republican candidate, Mitt Romney, but she quickly deleted it," New York Magazine's The Cut noted. Five years later, it remains her single public social media blunder—if you can call it that." According to the magazine, "Beyoncé Is the Leonardo da Vinci of Instagram." Beyoncé first established herself as a student of the arts. We frequently encountered photographs of her in galleries or museums. Artwork showed frequently in her stream. Years before her current Louvre music video, she was at the Louvre in October 2014, looking at La Joconde. She then evolved into the work of art itself. On many occasions, she demonstrated a strong affection for Warhol, including the posting of humorous multiple/mirror pictures of herself in her feed. "Imagine the power of 16 Beyoncés," Mashable wrote in 2017. Just imagine it. With that amount of power, you could provide a continent with robust, likely renewable electricity. And now we have a visual." With the death of fashion magazines, she presents a way forward for fashion photography in that medium, as well as through her own channels and very innovative videos. They're like small music videos, except they're all about Beyoncé's style.

She shot the video for "Apesh*t" in the Louvre in 2018, and her clothing was a literal portrayal of the museum's prominent pieces. Beyoncé's likeness to Marie-Guillemine Benoist's 1800 painting Portrait of a Black Woman (La Negresse) has been noted by art historian Theodore Barrow: "It is, in fact, a pretty rare depiction of a beautiful black woman in a mode that is closely tied to not only the depiction of the seated virgin Mary but also to mythological goddesses." Later that year, Bey's September 2018 Vogue cover was reminiscent of Jacques-Louis David's 1783 A Vestal Virgin Crowned with Flowers. Beyoncé's carefully crafted image addressed both how her supporters regard her as a goddess and how she encouraged her female fans to embrace their divine feminine. We may observe the coming of age of an icon in her usage of social media, one who remembers a youth without Twitter, Snapchat, or Instagram, but who is old enough and intelligent enough to master and remix the platforms.

Beyoncé's incredible sense of control over her imagery is an intriguing juxtaposition to the #metoo movement. One can only imagine that as a young artist, Beyoncé was aware of the difficulties that a female artist can face when the men in her professional life dominated her image. There is never a sense that Beyoncé is doing or exhibiting something she doesn't want to do, whether she is duplicating a beloved painting, posing with her family, or flashing a fashion-forward look.

It's worth mentioning that Instagram is only seven years old as a platform. Tumblr, Beyoncé's preferred platform before Instagram, is only 11 years old. However, Beyoncé has been in the public eye for more than two decades. In a relatively short period of time, she has broken the media chains that prevented an artist from directly communicating with their followers."To me, power is making things happen without asking for permission. It's affecting the way people perceive themselves and the world around them." As she told Elle magazine in 2016. Surprisingly, it is still uncommon to see a woman and an artist go through the world with as much power—and without the need or need for permission—as Beyoncé.

CHAPTER 10
The King of Pop and the Queen of All

Beyoncé symbolically grabbed the crown of best entertainer on the planet from Michael Jackson when, unfortunately, the curls atop her gorgeous crown were pulled into the blades of an electric fan. While that event had little to do with her rise, it did have a lot to do with the performance of a Black and female identity that could meet any challenge on any platform at any time while maintaining her dignity and cool.

On July 22, 2013, at the Bell Centre in Montreal, Canada, during the North American leg of her Mrs. Carter world tour, the same year she released Beyoncé, Beyoncé's golden locks became entangled in a circular high-powered fan as she descended stairs during an encore performance to get closer to her adoring audience. De Boer was joined by a security detail man and woman; the man offered de Boer a sharp instrument, and he was ultimately able to remove Beyoncé from the fan's remorseless suction. Beyoncé didn't miss a note and kept singing throughout, receiving a rousing cheer from her admirers once she was free.

It's not even that Beyoncé and Michael Jackson are an update on the gender inequality highlighted in a 1982 Frank and Ernest cartoon, which was memorably paraphrased by the late maverick treasurer and then-Texas governor Ann Richards at the 1988 Democratic National Convention when she said, "Ginger Rogers did everything that Fred Astaire did." She just did it in high heels and backwards." Beyoncé isn't simply repeating Michael Jackson's outstanding performance. She's doing something no one other has done before. She is a crafty maestro who, whether singing, dancing, or acting, leaves others in her wake. Michael's musical body of work is unparalleled, while Beyoncé's work as a singer-dancer-performer on stage and in videos as a singer-dancer-performer is unparalleled.

Beyoncé and Michael appeared to share a dynamic performance DNA passed down from Bill "Bojangles" Robinson to Josephine Baker, from Sammy Davis, Jr. to Katherine Dunham. Beyoncé attended her first performance at the age of six in April 1988, when she saw Michael Jackson perform at the Summit in Houston, Texas. Beyoncé spent numerous hours as a fledgling artist studying Michael Jackson videos, gleaning dancing techniques and ideas, as well as a grammar of elastic and electric entertainment. Beyoncé appreciated Michael Jackson's compelling performances, which featured a slim frame that expressed a flowing aesthetic of clean lines and mathematically precise motions. But she raised the stakes. Beyoncé's motion vocabulary grew as she developed, with a voluptuous form emphasizing a combustible physical expressiveness and a more intense poetry of flexibility.

Michael skillfully incorporated street dance into his act, most notably in his gigantic moonwalk, which bent time and crushed space in an optical illusion that appeared to reverse velocity and defy gravity.

He looked like Einstein in a fedora. Beyoncé feminizes flow geometry with her surrealistically supple limbs. In a regimen of fiercely maintained and wonderfully unresolved terpsichorean tensions: between formal and vernacular dance genres, ballet and hip hop, jazz and krumping, she brings sweet antagonism to her dance discipline.

Jackson appeared in public as an 11-year-old prodigy, a little adult seemingly immune to small chat and child's play. His vocals erupted in a sonic volcano, burying his youth beneath an unbelievable, enticing expertise. He may have known too much for his age, but he may also have known too much for his own benefit. Jackson's work provided a window into feelings that he could never have comprehended.

Beyoncé had an equally active and engaged childhood in Houston, albeit in a significantly more stable environment than the working-class Jackson family in Gary, Indiana. Beyoncé is the daughter of former sales representative Matthew and former cosmetologist Tina, who raised Beyoncé and her younger sister, Solange, in relative comfort. Beyoncé was shy and had few friends when she was seven years old, so her parents enrolled her in a dancing class. Matthew and Tina were taken aback a short time later at a community event when they saw Beyoncé sing and dance with a confidence and energy they had never seen in her before.

Beyoncé, like Michael, was most alive on stage, and she, like him, found her esteem and métier in performance, in the public display of privately cherished joys through song and dance. Beyoncé competed in and won numerous talent shows and beauty pageants. She joined the singing group Girls Tyme when she was nine, displaying her precocious talent and prodigious work ethic while learning to compartmentalize the personal and professional, a trait that famously survived her teenage years as a star in the phenomenal girl group Destiny's Child, the successor to Girls Tyme, and into adulthood with her legendary solo career.

It's also worth noting what Michael and Beyoncé did with their vocals. Michael's drive to explore the depths of his voice as a child harkened back to Mozart's early genius. His soaring, emotional arpeggios as he sped up and down scales like a music track star; his sorrowful moaning, cooing, and humming that formed a golden tunnel of sound through which his notes found glorious escape; and his raw crying and brave vulnerability were all hallmarks of his vocal wizardry. Jackson wrote a series of pop songs that revolutionized American music while avoiding racial stereotypes. Jackson achieved his commercial apex with 1982's Thriller, the world's best selling record of all time, after embellishing disco, fomenting funk, and dabbling in light rock on his outstanding 1979 album Off the Wall.

As talented as Michael Jackson was as a singer—Jackson, for example, stylistically echoed James Brown and Jackie Wilson, as well as Otis Redding and William Hart—Beyoncé has surpassed him with her ecstatic experimentalism, which has sparked her stylistic evolution of off-kilter syncopations, rhizomes of jutting rhythms layered atop one another, and the fertile fusion of talk-rap singing. Beyoncé is probably the matriarch and forefather of the mumble rap style, if not in terms of content or topics, then in terms of sinuous, esoteric phrasing and masking panache that revels in elided syllables; blurred, then merged, consonants; and conjoined, or contrapuntal, ellipses.

Michael's most dynamic, explosive vocal performances, both on record and on stage, took place between the ages of eight and twenty-one, when the colossal weight of his transcendent singing skills gave way to an airier sonic shimmer that he cleverly preserved in a softer and higher register of notes. When Michael fully realized his creative genius as an auteur, he lost the range and resonance of his more brutally soulful and bluesy sound.

Beyoncé, on the other hand, has progressed from vocal prodigy to master, exploring a hazardous sonic landscape that has only gained its range, depth, and force. In her acoustic topography, Beyoncé's voice unleashes a cascade of notes down mountains of styles, some jagged with delightfully angry hip hop beats that disdain linear rhythms, others smoothed in R&B melodies and harmonies that form an archipelago of gospel grooves. Michael on stage, singing, after achieving global renown, is no match for Beyoncé on stage, singing, after achieving international acclaim. The sheer quality of sound flowing from her durable instrument long into her forties elevates

Beyoncé above Michael and her contemporaries. Beyoncé is in a league of her own when the sparkling range of her song meets the wild freedom of her body on stage.

Michael started the Jackson 5 singing ensemble with four of his siblings in 1968, the same year Martin Luther King, Jr. was assassinated. Beginning in 1969, their run of singles ushered in a post-civil rights version of Blackness that exploded on record with their electric sound and on stage with their trendy show of race pride. He and his brothers portrayed Black masculinity with the style of the Black Panthers and the broad appeal of Tony the Tiger, which is why their own cartoon series—their animation artistry—aided in the integration of Saturday-morning television in the early 1970s. Although it was bubblegum, their Blow Pops were spiked: The Jackson 5 showed an intact unit whose image of unity was as revolutionary in its own right as what was happening in the courts and streets, only a few years after the Moynihan Report had stated in 1965 that the Black family was in shambles. Without protest or resistance, blacks and whites rode Michael Jackson's vocal cords into musical ecstasy and accepted the gentle racial theology of Motown universalism.

Beyoncé's Blackness has been complicated and contested since her childhood, when she was bullied at school because of her light skin and hair, to her adulthood, when her racial identity and gender politics have been relentlessly questioned, both within Black life and feminist circles and far beyond. Beyoncé's Blackness has been subtle and subversive, implicit and explicit, central and incidental, practically accidental, both taken for granted and rendered invisible, or at the very least benign.

In the white world, her pop style has been viewed or understood as non-Black, nonracial, global, and transcendent. She is a language, a medium, an identity, a category of existence and consciousness of her own; she is Beyoncé, a language, a medium, an identity, a category of existence and consciousness all her own. Her Black acts, on the other hand, have occasionally shattered the compact of racelessness for a Black artist in America, namely, that they swear off any hint of Blackness and instead view Blackness as instrumental, that is, as critical in realizing the means to an artistic end, rather than substantive, that is, as grounding both one's approach and music—and one's themes, ideas, and identity, and even one's politics—in that Blackness.

All of this worry about Beyoncé arose following her meteoric rise to prominence. The more successful she grew, the more she controlled global media, art, and culture, the less Black she appeared to whites in the United States and around the world. Beyoncé conquered one of the most formidable obstacles to Blackness: whiteness, which fantasizes that its racial identity is neutral and its ideals are universal. Even the Black object of white fancy becomes a lifestyle, a goal, an aspiration, and, finally, an image of perfection unblemished by any particular identity in such a culture. Such an illusory image can only be addressed if one is willing to fight the parameters of elevation and reject the projection of political ideals onto one's body that such a status bestows. One must be willing to embrace an identity that is considered as unqualified for cultural deification: a dirty, dark, polluted Blackness that physically emerges from the dust of Western civilisation to transform society and culture.

The rejected stone of Blackness, to paraphrase the Bible, has become the cornerstone of a civilisation that was skeptical of its worth and merit. Beyoncé's body is a busy intersection where dangerous collisions occur between the cranky specificity of a Blackness rooted in the skin and skill of everyday Black folk and, from the other direction, a colonized and curtailed Blackness, a fetishized and toothless Blackness, a subservient and symbolic Blackness.

While Beyoncé is largely regarded as the world's greatest star, she has experienced her own form of artistic apartheid. Despite winning a slew of Grammys, she has been denied the most prestigious prizes, including Record and Album of the Year. Following the release of her seminal album Lemonade—a dizzying amalgam of musical genres, Black cultural allusions and references, Black iconography, carnal and spiritual desires, African female deities, serpentine phrases, trap beats, staccato cadences, and existential and institutional marital angst—all in the service of channeling rage at social inequities, particularly the machinery of toxic masculinities and traitorous patriarchies, in defense of vulnerable-turned-vBeyoncé has received nine Grammy nominations, including Album, Record, and Song of the Year.

The Recording Academy didn't drink the Lemonade; the excellent album was snubbed for the top prizes, winning only Best Music Video and Best Urban Contemporary Album. Beyoncé was ghettoized and given an award to match the official musical culture's estimation of her value in a year in which her artistic genius soared, shattered conceptual barriers, and transgressed social boundaries, as if to remind her of the narrow definitions of Blackness in which she should remain cocooned.

Recognizing the significance of Blackness in the art one consumes is insufficient if the worth of Black art to the American enterprise is not recognized. Giving Beyoncé a Grammy for Best Urban Contemporary while denying her recognition for her American genius with specific Grammy prizes that transcend genre is a disrespect to her Blackness and an oblique disregard for her Americanness.

Perhaps that underlying insight prompted Michael Jackson's attempts in radical self-reimagining to a large extent. Michael altered his face in his own image, the one ingrained in his mind as a child by a father who tormented him about being ugly. Jackson began to believe that he was overly dark and had a big nose. His constant self-mutilation through reconstructive surgery was a harsh expression of the self-hatred that cuts the Black psyche. Although Jackson claimed to have vitiligo, a disorder that causes skin to lose pigment, he may have bleached his skin to remove the objectionable Blackness from his face.

Beyoncé's pale complexion has also played a role in her life, in her public perception, and in the colorism politics that follow her. "Sometimes, in the black community, it's the lighter girls who are picked on," Beyoncé's mother, Tina Lawson, explained. "Of course, the opposite is frequently true as well—the darker girls are also targeted." It's unfortunate, but it's a reality of life. Despite Michael's risky skin politics, it was easy to perceive the Blackness and magnificence of the music he created, as well as the broad humanity of the globally popular kind of entertainment he championed. Michael Jackson did not receive the nurturing, love, and unconditional affirmation he desired from his father during his early infancy. When Michael Jackson died at the age of 50, our only solace was that Prince, the other Black musical prodigy born in the Midwest the same year as Jackson, was still strutting the earth in trendy platforms.

His Royal Badness' death on April 21, 2016, just as Beyoncé poured her next musical elixir on the world on April 23, 2016, lacked the astrology and area synchronization that molded his delicate rivalry with the King of Pop.

Despite their instructive differences, Prince and Beyoncé, as well as Michael, remind us that the pieties of faith torch and heal the flesh, that musical boundaries, as well as those between the political and personal, can be brilliantly transgressed, and that extravagant performances of race and gender, as well as sexual identity, frequently threaten power's and monoculture vain sovereignty. Beyoncé now reigns alone, atop a kingdom of performance that she inherited from a Prince and a King but has expanded. Beyoncé's astonishing career symbolizes the clash of violent race and gender dynamics while she reigns as the world's most magnificent performer. Beyoncé has managed to command the artistic respect of her peers as well as the adoration of millions of fans all over the world while expressing her unique brand of feminism: the insistence that women's lives matter, that their issues matter, that they be treated with respect, and that women achieve social and economic equality. Beyoncé's formidable fusion politics—of musical styles and rhythms, Black female deities and cultural icons, material aspirations and spiritual desires—has bolstered her expansion of Black artistic identity by embracing queer sensibilities, amplifying progressive racial interpretations of Black suffering, and centering existence in a Black female worldview.

Beyoncé is the greatest performer of all time because she has absorbed and extended Michael Jackson's best attributes and wisest lessons in her ever-evolving, tirelessly shapeshifting drive for excellence. Whether she is singing, dancing, rapping, making videos or documentaries, or using her art to protest, rally, signify, edify, and, most importantly, entertain, Beyoncé is an outsize genius whose quest for greatness has blazed a path that no one before her has traveled and, without a doubt, few, if any, after her can successfully pursue.

CHAPTER 11
Beyoncé the Fearless

In the 1980s, I grew up in Schaumburg, Illinois. I used to despise the color of my skin. I wished my mother wouldn't be wearing a sari to the neighborhood Kmart. When my friends came over and my house smelled like Indian cooking, I was mortified. I didn't know who I was back then. Every day was another day of trying to fit in, to appear, talk, and act like the others. Something changed on the last day of eighth grade. Another classmate made a nasty remark about me, and for the first (and last) time, I got into a physical fight after school. I was terribly beaten, yet I was happy to wear that black eye. I was proud of myself for not backing down from a fight. That was the day I began exploring my Indian identity and seeking out people who looked like me. I was resurrected to fight for inclusivity and the most vulnerable individuals. That's when I began to feel proud of myself.

No matter how famous or wealthy Beyoncé has become, she has never let anyone forget where she came from or who she is. That, to me, is being a true role model. I met Beyoncé twice: once at a Michelle Obama dinner at an Italian restaurant in the West Village, and again in 2013 at the Justice for Trayvon Martin rally. Backstage at the rally, I was in a prayer circle with about a dozen other individuals, including Beyoncé and Jay-Z. It was an experience I'll never forget. We were just a bunch of parents and kids who were hurting and healing in our neighborhood. Beyoncé did not appear as Queen Bey, but as a mother, and particularly as a Black mother. She and Jay-Z attended the rally out of love for the lives of young boys like Trayvon, who were and continue to be murdered in our streets.

I present myself completely. I discuss my background and my refugee parents. I discuss my name, Reshma, and how I refused to change it when I stood for public office in 2010.

Like Beyoncé, when my platform grows, I will say more about who I am and where I came from. I want other dark females to see themselves in my story and in the world of technology. Culture has done an excellent job of convincing girls and women, particularly those who are not white, that they belong in certain settings but not in others. They should be successful, but not overly so. They should work solely in specific fields and not in others.

I have faith that things will improve. We've already seen a lot of development and energy focused on women's empowerment. Beyoncé has played an important role in that advancement for myself and many other girls and women. She has always pushed me to push myself as a leader and as a woman. We had a group of eight women, largely women of color, at Yale who would listen to "Survivor" and her other songs of vulnerability and courage on repeat. Sixteen years later, I still listen to her music when I want to feel powerful before delivering a speech. And I sometimes need to feel powerful even when I'm not onstage.

I have a disease that causes repeated miscarriages. Between 2012 and 2014, I went through a really dark phase in my life, suffering from several of them. Every time my husband and I went to the hospital for a checkup at the start of a pregnancy, it seemed to end in disaster. We'd walk into the appointment room, eager to see the sonogram and hear a heartbeat that, inevitably, wasn't there. It was more of the same the fourth time I became pregnant: appointments and waiting in cold exam rooms for news. Except that this time, the music was Beyoncé's "XO." It has a statement about seeing someone in the darkness. That touched my heart. I imagined seeing my child and loving him so much that I would be with him through this darkness one day. That song gave me hope and strength. It helped me get over my terrible times.

When Beyoncé opened up about her loss in her documentary, and then about her pregnancy with twins in Vogue—the emergency C-section, the difficult recovery, her shifting body—it meant so lot to me and so many other women I know. That is what we seek in those we admire: genuineness. We desire imperfections, and we want to know that they, like us, have overcome obstacles and prospered. Beyoncé's honesty and sensitivity are what make her both relatable and iconic.

I talk a lot about the need for bravery in this perfectionist culture, about how females are socialized to be perfect, discouraged from failing, and discouraged from being brave. I began to be brave when I began to embrace my Indian identity, then again when I campaigned for political office twice and lost both times, and then again when I really desired a child but was repeatedly disappointed. My world did not end every time I chose bravery. I was able to stand up and keep going every time, even when it seemed impossible. I always came out stronger. Beyoncé inspired that fearlessness in me back then, and she continues to do it now. She embodies what it means to be a brave, if not perfect, woman. We all adore her for it.

CHAPTER 12
Living into the Lemonade: Redefining Black Women's Spirituality in Beyoncé's Era

Yes, she is an international superstar, but many people overlook the fact that Beyoncé is a Southern church girl immersed in Black church aesthetics and customs. While her music and iconic reputation celebrate her unashamed sexuality, she has not deviated from the directions given to church girls in her personal life. Beyoncé married Jay before having Blue, following the path that the religion promised would lead to endless bliss and contentment. Nothing is more important than obedience to God, as Black Southern females are well aware. It is the cornerstone for a prosperous existence. But what if your entire achievement violates everything the religion taught us? Beyoncé is a difficult figure in the eyes of the church. On the one hand, she married and started a family, as all good Christian girls are taught.

Beyoncé's solo career was our twenties' soundtrack. We were familiar with her. We grew up beside her. She was the attractive girl on the dance team in high school. The guys adored her. None of the females wanted to, but her goodness outweighed her beauty, and she was simply too sweet to dislike. We Southern girls understood better than to believe that God desired a healthy sexual identity for us. However, as a generation nurtured equally by the Black church and hip hop, these messages simply do not hold up under inspection and common reason. We still wanted to be nice girls, balancing what we "knew" was right and what we felt. Beyonce assisted us with that trip during her Destiny's Child days and at the start of her solo career.

We always received that one mandatory gospel song on DC CDs. My pals and I referred to it as the "Jesus track." And on Bey's earliest solo releases, even if the songs weren't strictly gospel, they were church-related enough to be sung by the youth choir at a Sunday service. These songs all served to demonstrate that, despite Beyoncé's sexual prowess, she hadn't strayed too far from her Christian roots. Those within the Southern Black church culture understood the significance of such a pronouncement.

We were instructed as Southern church ladies to avoid suggestive and explicit music. We were never to sing or perform anything that would lead our brethren to sin. That was just not something good girls did. We were meant to be poised and chaste, and Beyoncé knew this as a religious kid. Despite this, we witnessed her popping and dropping, dropping hit after hit to assist us polish our twerk and complain. But she didn't abandon us without a fight. If the rest of the record made us sin on Saturday night, we knew we'd be able to sing at least one song as we drove into the church parking lot on Sunday morning.

Beyoncé's theological training was more progressive than most, thanks to her upbringing at St. John's United Methodist Church in Northwest Houston. Beyoncé's church, known for spreading a gospel of tolerance and acceptance, provided many messages about faith and sexuality—messages that would definitely affect both her personal relationship with God and her professional career. Despite her progressive theological upbringing, Beyoncé was unable to avoid the schism between Black women's spiritual and sexual identities. We don't know how she dealt with the internal conflict. However, as church girls, many of us saw those "Jesus tracks" and Sasha Fierce as Beyoncé's attempts to traverse the liminal area between fully claiming her emerging pop icon status and establishing that she was still the same sweet girl from Houston.

We all work so hard to please others, and Beyoncé's likability stemmed in part from her ability to separate her sexuality from her spirit. Yes, she had a wanton sexuality on stage, but she was a decent Southern lady raised on Jesus and sweet tea in real life. Living two lives may be exhausting for anyone. Since the birth of Blue Ivy, we'd seen glimpses of this newfound self-determination, but Beyoncé took things to an unexpected level. Many thought she had something to prove. Perhaps she did. Others perceived her as bored of following the rules. That was as if Beyoncé was saying that she could be all of these things within herself—erotic, maternal, political, and spiritual—and that if someone had a problem with that, it was their problem, not hers.

Just as IV's declaration of freedom cleared the path for Beyoncé's absolute liberty, Lemonade's heavenly magic did as well. Beyoncé admits that betrayal has penetrated her home, and in order to cope, she turns to what she knows best: God and the church. She finds herself at the altar, praying with God to provide a way—a place she has visited before with her own mother. Beyoncé follows the guidelines she's been given in order to withstand these difficult times as a responsible Christian woman. She has put so much of herself in a love that has damaged her, and her reaction is understandable. We're taught in church to give it to God; wrath cannot exist in the heart of a woman who is completely committed to her religion. Beyoncé rejects this in Lemonade. It is possible to love God passionately while yet having a strong, human reaction to the hurt caused by individuals we trust. There is room for us to live fully into our humanity. We've seen women in our families and congregations deny their feelings in order to appease a God who simply wants honesty. Beyoncé's generation of church girls will offer that to God and the world, creating our own Lemonade in ways that contradict much of what we've been taught.

Because of orthodox Christianity's contentious and inconsistent messages about Black womanhood and sexuality, I honestly feel that Black women's spirituality cannot be fully realized in the mainstream church. Lemonade represents the peace that many Black women have experienced after accepting this. Beyoncé elevated the Christian God and the Oshun in the same work, demonstrating how she belongs to a long line of Black women who have forged their own spiritual liberties. Those mothers and sages live by their own set of rules and continually encourage us to follow suit. Not only in Beyoncé's art, but also in her life, do we see the fruits of their knowledge. Beyoncé demonstrated to those who wanted her to leave that it is possible to stay and fight for something beautiful. Mrs. Knowles-Carter reminded her husband of her power and made him work for it, despite others who wanted her to pretend as if nothing had happened. Above all, the icon demonstrated that the death of her Sasha Fierce alter ego and the independence that began with the IV album were not marketing tricks. She is unique. She is always true to herself and encourages us to do the same.

Many Black women grew thirsty after viewing Lemonade for what would allow them to remain in such an informed and transparent atmosphere. Many of us who were live tweeting the HBO premiere were inspired by the film's Black feminist and womanist themes. Lemonade elicited feelings that Black women had previously suppressed or refused to accept, and we needed to address them. It certainly did for me. It created room for me to be honest about my sorrow, consider new options, and develop my own healing and wholeness. I'm grateful that it had the same effect on other ladies. To work through the Lemonade Syllabus in its entirety, Black women across the country formed Lemonade Syllabus book clubs.

Lemonade Syllabus courses have been developed at universities that will examine the Syllabus as a Black feminist work, as well as Lemonade and Beyoncé's broader cultural impact. There have also been Lemonade Syllabus "stands" at public libraries, where I've had the opportunity to talk on the worldwide significance of Black feminist and womanist literature. Great art is both inspiring and transforming. We are not living in a post-Lemonade era. We are, more accurately, living into it. If we are to completely apply Lemonade's lessons, we must first leave the places that have damaged us. This is not restricted to personal relationships amongst Black women. Black women are negotiating death-dealing professional and spiritual relationships, and Lemonade is giving us permission to leave if we need it. And our reaction to Lemonade directs us toward the Lemonade itself.

When Black women choose to live in the Lemonade, they choose a joy that will not be reduced by the violence that will continue to be directed at them. It's the delight of Grandma's cooking table, where she will nourish your starving body and wounded spirit. It is the joy of Black hair salons, where Black women provide each other with momentary sanctuary from the harsh realities of Black existence in America. Every Beyoncé world tour, Black women describe their experience as spiritual, claiming she took them to church. Black women have always found ways to live into the Lemonade, and if sisters are to thrive in the future, this must become our default position. We've all worked hard to recover from traumatic situations, and we deserve to celebrate that. Those lemons, however tart, are not the conclusion of the story. Despite them, we created something; we created a life—a wonderful one. Here's to savoring each drink.

CHAPTER 13
Beyoncé's Radical Ways

Beyoncé is a clever, underrated force in terms of political identity. Given her prominence and accessibility, she has been able to bring radicalism to the forefront of public discourse in unprecedented ways. We need change agents to march and protest, but we also need someone to take the movement mainstream, which she has done time and again. She is using her platform to raise awareness of critical social issues such as police brutality and feminism.

I needed a "day job," so I began working with young people who were incarcerated or had previously been incarcerated, attempting to help them find their voice. I started organizing cultural and spiritual ceremonies and programs such as Juneteenth, Cinco de Mayo, and pow wows inside the Deuel Vocational Institution, also known as Tracy prison, for men who were facing life sentences through an organization called Barrios Unidos. I met my mentor, Nane Alejandrez, through this work, and he eventually introduced me to Mr. Belafonte. I was brought in as a mentee in a bigger conversation about eliminating child incarceration as a moral necessity. Mr. Belafonte was introduced to me while I was attending those meetings.

He was constructing a movement based on Kingian nonviolence, Dr. King's doctrine, as the foundation for civic involvement, political action, and transforming the narrative around young incarceration. And he invited me to accompany him. I initially joined The Gathering for Justice as national organizing director to assist establish the organization. Since becoming executive director in 2010, I've established two state-based task forces, Justice League NYC and now Justice League CA, to coordinate activism around crucial legislative improvements to reduce mass incarceration.

Between Mr. Belafonte's legacy, The Gathering for Justice, and Justice League, we are able to connect influencers to issues that affect the lives of Black and brown people, particularly when it comes to incarceration, police, and women's rights.

Beyoncé has historically used her art to convey political messages, which she backs up with tangible activism. The personal is absolutely political for her. She identifies as a feminist and represents Black brilliance; she has assembled an exceptional team of largely women of color—from the stage to the office—creating economic and creative opportunities for underprivileged people. Her humanitarian activism is purposefully aimed at lifting up all women, but especially Black women. She exemplifies feminism by saying, "I can both challenge and uplift the men in my community." Beyoncé is subtle and eloquent: inclusive, purposeful, and intersectional, and in this way she models new ways of being for feminist women like myself.

Lemonade was a strong combination of activism, power, and vulnerability, all delivered in savage amounts. Because of the anguish, fury, and resilience she conveyed, so many of us could connect. Liberation music, in my opinion, is art that affects and uplifts our various and intersecting identities. Beyoncé also appears in popular areas where these daring debates are still needed. She enters the homes of many Americans who have never had a dialogue about Black Lives Matter or feminism. For example, she used the Super Bowl to bring the topic of police brutality to the forefront of public discourse.

Mr. B delivered an outstanding statement on gun control at the 2013 NAACP Image Awards. He spoke of the blood of Black youngsters spilling across America's streets. He urged the church, lawmakers, and the community to take action. In part, he said:

The group that is most devastated by America's obsession with guns is African Americans. Although making comparisons can be dangerous, there are times when they must be noted. America has the largest prison population in the world, and of the over two million men, women and children who make up the incarcerated, the overwhelming majority of them are black. African Americans are the most unemployed, the most caught in the unjust systems of justice. And in the gun game, they are the most hunted. The rivers of blood that wash the streets of our nation flow mostly from the bodies of our black children. Yet, as the great debate emerges on the question of the gun, white America discusses the constitutional issues of ownership, while no one speaks to the consequences of our racial carnage. Where is the outraged voice of black America? Where? And why are we mute? Where are our leaders? Where are our legislators? Where is the church?

Jamie Foxx was expected to accept an award immediately following Mr. B's remarks. But he practically couldn't speak when Mr. Belafonte finished speaking, such was the impact of his speech on him. Following his lecture, Jamie Foxx, Talib Kweli, Common, John Legend, and others sought mentorship and advice from Mr. B on how to construct a creative life that is more firmly and successfully founded in activism. Mr. B also chatted with Jesse Williams, Dave Chappelle, and a slew of other influential people. This has rekindled the kinds of relationships that were fostered during the Civil Rights Movement, and the Gathering for Justice has created a body of work based on that history of connecting artists and movement builders.

This era has also been ushered in by a singular convergence of technology and the emergence of social media as a tool for concerned and engaged individuals. Because we have information at the tips of our fingers thanks to social media and video cameras incorporated into all of our phones, each individual tale in the killings of unarmed black and brown people by police cannot be downplayed or rationalized by the powers that be as in the past. As people of color in this nation, police brutality has long been a part of our story. The difference now is that, because of technological means such as smartphones and social media, we may circumvent media gatekeepers and openly bear witness to crimes perpetrated.

Mr. Belafonte's criticism of Jay-Z and Beyoncé for not being socially responsible as celebrities with wealth and influence was utterly misconstrued. He didn't want to diminish their work, but he maintained that we hadn't seen many artists of their caliber take a visible stand on any of these problems. Our company connects the stars to the people on the ground. T.I., for example, may text me to inquire about organizations working on the frontlines when an incident occurs in a given town. People are sometimes hesitant to take a prominent political stance because it may backfire. Colin Kaepernick has been blacklisted as a result of his political stance. I admire his bravery in doing the right thing despite the consequences. "When we speak, we are afraid that our words will not be heard or welcomed," Audre Lorde once wrote. But even when we remain silent, we are terrified. So it is preferable to speak."

Beyoncé is an inspiration because she speaks up, skillfully using her own stage and platform to magnify messages of Black liberation and Black excellence. You have to pay attention to the cultural moments that are happening at the same time: there is a big sense of pride in having Beyoncé at Coachella and playing the Black National Anthem. The motivation she has provided for so many young women of color is just incalculable.

I believe Beyoncé has always been political, but no one noticed until recently. They didn't notice because her music is quite mainstream, and you have to listen carefully to see that there is a radicalism in her honesty and these indie windows of subliminal messages. She is extremely discreet. Even her friendship with Jay was initially kept hidden. She has, nevertheless, made an unexpected shift into politics. The distinction between her and other artists is that she has been very deliberate in terms of where her platform has been used, how it has been used, and what she has been messaging. Speaking your views and speaking directly to people of color and women in public requires a certain level of power. Mr. Belafonte has lived long enough and seen enough to have a thorough historical analysis and a very distinct viewpoint on the current political atmosphere. That's why, at 91 years old, he's still relevant, why he's such a tremendous advisor and mentor to so many. What I admire about Beyoncé is how she's been extremely clever in her activism—she's not considered a lefty, yet look at how radical her imagery and lyrics can be. I can't wait to see her develop and mature by the time she reaches Mr. B's age.

CHAPTER 14
La Reina can be found in Queen Bey

It wasn't until the third time I met Beyoncé that she revealed her superpower to me. I just said hello the first two times, in the late 1990s, at record industry meet-and-greets when Destiny's Child was working hard to get fans to mention their names. The third and fourth occasions were a decade later, in 2008 and 2011, respectively, by which time Beyoncé had achieved recognized solo status, both as an artist and as a name, and I interviewed her for cover stories for InStyle magazine, where I worked as an editor.

I was scared and new to my position the first time I met with her, as well as emotionally fragile, having just lost my mother a few weeks before. My first true superstar interview was with Beyoncé. I recall exactly what I wore because I gave it a lot of thought, as you should when meeting an artist you've long loved. I glanced at my list of unasked questions at the end of our permitted hour, sitting next to her on a black leather couch in the industrial photo studio, and realized I wasn't going to have time to get to them. I don't believe I appeared flustered, but she picked up on my worry. When a handler arrived to end the session, Beyoncé informed her that everything was good and that she should give us more time. "Go ahead," she said, "ask whatever you need to." I took a deep breath and thanked her. Every time I've met her, she's been kind, but with interpersonal limits that reflect the hardworking professional she is: firm handshakes, persistent eye contact, and focus and attention to the questions. She is serious, yet she is also friendly, smiles frequently, and is quick to laugh at herself. What struck me the most was how supportive she was of me, and it's because of this that I know her sisterhood is genuine, that she genuinely is a woman's woman. During the interview, I also learnt that her best friend is Cuban, just like me, and that she enjoys Latin culture and food. It hit me because, as a Latina, I've always admired her appearance. From a young age, I was taught to notice and adore women who dress nicely, wear makeup and high heels, and display feminine silhouettes—signifiers I've always identified as specific to the Latin environment I grew up in. It's all about the lipstick, the accessories, and the leg-lengthening stilettos.

Beyoncé told me in that first interview that she didn't feel dressed without big earrings, that she loves platform heels, and that her mother—who comes from a Creole family from Caribbean-influenced southern Louisiana and grew up on the Gulf in Galveston, Texas—made sure she and her sister Solange always had their blush or lip gloss in their purses. It doesn't get more Latin than devotion to lip gloss and a mother's rage at leaving the house undone. "When you look at beauty and the Southern black girl, it can be indistinguishable from beauty as presented in Dominican or Cuban culture," says Zandria Robinson, an Africana Studies expert. "There is a shared emphasis on beauty, elegance, femininity, and self-presentation."

This particular brand of beauty and femininity is evident in Beyoncé's album artwork, videos, and social media accounts, and there has been speculation about her visual embrace of West African deities who influence and define the spiritual aspects of the Latin Caribbean region, from Santeria in Cuba to Candomblé in Brazil. Aside from her physical appearance, Beyoncé has long been a fan of Latin music: She performed with Destiny's Child on the Latin Grammys in 2002, alongside Spanish crooner and global superstar Alejandro Sanz; in 2006, she released an EP of Spanish covers from B'Day, including "Amor Gitano" with famed Mexican singer Alejandro Fernández, which was used as the theme song for a beloved Zorro-themed telenovela; and in 2008, she released a Spanish version of "If I Were a Boy." Her biggest Spanish-language hit last year, however, was a remix of Colombian reggaeton sensation J. Balvin and French DJ and producer Willy William's global dance smash "Mi Gente." It spent 30 weeks on the Billboard Hot 100, peaking at number three. She donated the song's revenues to disaster relief efforts in Puerto Rico, Mexico, and the Caribbean, which were heavily struck by Hurricanes Irma and Maria.

As a gangly Cuban teenager growing up in Atlanta in the 1980s, my musical tastes were influenced by MTV videos (Whitney, Madonna, Michael) and my parents' vinyl collection. From Willie to Aretha, Stevie to Billy, and, of course, Gloria and Celia, the dual patron saints of Cuban music, their taste was varied but cool. Despite the fact that my parents were born on the island, Latin music was not the sole soundtrack of their adult lives in Atlanta, and it was not my soundtrack growing up as one of the few Latin students in my school. I didn't have a stronger sense of pride or faithful listening until I was in my twenties, when I visited my brother in South Beach. Music is ubiquitous in Miami, blasting from cars and boats throughout the day and blaring from clubs at night, where we'd go to dance to techno, house, and Latin music. At my brother's house, I spent quieter moments learning about Benny Moré and La Lupe from his record collection. But it was Miami in the mid-1990s, when Gianni Versace was throwing extravagant parties at his Ocean Drive villa and introducing the world to Albita. I had begun to become aware of the history, influence, and richness of Latin music, but the rest of the country, with the exception of pockets of New York, Texas, and California, was still a few years away from recognizing it as the hot sound. That's one of the reasons I'm so excited that history is being made as I write this in the summer of 2018: Cardi B, nee Belcalis Almánzar, a Dominican American stripper-turned-reality star-turned-urban artist, has become the first female rapper to have two number one singles on the Billboard Hot 100. Her first single, the Louboutin-loving "Bodak Yellow (Money Moves)," peaked in October of that year, and now she's charting with "I Like It," an urban spin on Pete Rodriguez's legendary Nuyorican smash from the late 1960s. And, while Cardi isn't breaking any records for being the first Latina to reach the top of the world's most important music consumption chart (Jennifer Lopez did it four times, the last time with 2003's "All I Have"), it's a significant accomplishment on a chart that frequently features non-Latinos and songs in English. "I Like It" is primarily performed in Spanish, thanks to appearances by Bad Bunny of Puerto Rico and J. Balvin of Colombia.

It is the first number one for both Balvin and Bunny, but Balvin came close last year with the Beyoncé remix of "Mi Gente." The song was already gaining traction before Beyoncé—and her daughter Blue, who contributes four lyrics to the track—joined in. But her participation, in Spanish no less, propelled it to the top of the charts and gave it the ultimate sign of approval from tastemakers. Its popularity has also been aided by recent audience receptivity to Latin music's crossover appeal: in 2014, Enrique Iglesias, Descemer Bueno, and Gente de Zona broke records with their ubiquitous urban pop Spanish-language song "Bailando," and in 2017, Luis Fonsi,

Daddy Yankee, and Justin Bieber broke even more records with "Despacito," including becoming the first song ever to receive five billion views on YouTube.

Beyoncé's admirers, Latino and non-Latino alike, adored it and showed their support, notably on Twitter, where they jokingly conjugated her name into a Spanish grammar lesson. It's no surprise that Tommy Mottola, the chairman and CEO of Sony Music at the time, who signed Destiny's Child in 1996, was involved in the Latin Grammy performance, which he helped CBS start in 2000. Mottola grew up in the Bronx, where "Tito Puente was as much a part of the musical fabric as pop and rock 'n roll," according to him. As Sony's CEO, he ushered in the late 1990s Latin wave by signing and pushing out Shakira, Ricky Martin, Jennifer Lopez, Marc Anthony, and Gloria Estefan. He was also the driving force behind the Latin Explosion in 1999, when Latin musicians such as Ricky Martin and Jennifer Lopez all charted in the top ten on Billboard's Hot 100 with Latin-tinged English-language songs.

Beyoncé Giselle Knowles-Carter was born and raised in Houston, a city steeped in Latin—particularly Mexican—culture, food, and music. Hispanics make up over half of the population, and the population is expected to be majority Hispanic within four years. It's where Spanish is spoken on the streets, Latin music is always on the radio, and Tejana star Selena Quintanilla set attendance records at the Astrodome. Beyoncé revealed in a 2007 interview with People en Espanol that a close Mexican friend in Houston initially exposed her to Selena's records, which she then "listened to all the time." She consulted a close Cuban friend before recording songs in Spanish to ensure her accent sounded authentic.

Anyone else who attempts what Robinson refers to as Beyoncé's synchronism of so many cultures risks coming out as opportunistic. Beyoncé is not one of them. "When you sing in Spanish and try on our culture, you run the risk of someone saying you're not doing it right and aren't talking to us," explains Leila Cobo, Billboard's executive director of Latin Content. "Beyoncé has never faced such backlash." Beyoncé, like Cole, excels at her trade and works hard to improve it, whether it's hours of diction instruction with Luis Fonsi's brother Jean Rodriguez for "Mi Gente," or making sure her best friend, a Cuban, approves of how she sings a Spanish love ballad. Respect is evident. "She sees the music as being really good music, artistically interesting, and having its own merit," Cobo explains. "She doesn't consider Latin to be a passing fad." It's not a passing craze, and I'm all for it. The Latino community is rising across the country and is young (according to the Pew Research Center, approximately 60% of U.S. Hispanics are millennials), which means we are driving trends. Latin musicians and Spanish-language songs are charting higher and more frequently than in past years, and streaming data shows that Latin songs are popular (two of Spotify's top five global playlists are Latin). Of course, the fact that Latin music is increasingly being categorized helps.

CHAPTER 15
Style So Sacred

They were dressed in jeans. Jeans that are extremely tight. I first watched Destiny's Child perform at London's Notting Hill Carnival. They were all dressed similarly. I only remember their skintight jeans, not their tops. I had initially heard their first album a few months before, which I had played on repeat. They were all fantastic, but I knew Beyoncé was going to be a superstar. Beyoncé, beyond her voice, talents, and appearance, is someone who has had to work hard and strives for perfection. You can tell she worked hard to become who she is now. I appreciate and respect that aspect of her personality because nothing was delivered to me on a silver platter. And, while refining your craft is important, it's not just the music that made her—it's also about looking fantastic and the fashion choices she made with each song. Her fashion choices have always been well-considered. That was evident from the start, with the daring and seductive looks in "Independent Women" and the synchronized army fatigues in "Survivor."

I knew she was going to be a fashion heavyweight when I heard her solo album, Dangerously in Love. The styling of those videos—"Crazy in Love," "Bonnie and Clyde"—hypersexy but never vulgar, streetwear but also designer, that ideal high-low combination, amazing hair and makeup, and her forceful attitude all contributed to her transformation into a true fashion star at the time. That was when I believed she truly married her music and fashion. Fashion is always a reflection of the times we live in. Consider Lemonade, which conveys tremendous messages of independence and feminism through song and design, all of which are centered on women. One of my favorite outfits is the feminine red, white, and black script-print silk Gucci dress she wears on top of the police cruiser.

I was the creative director of W magazine at the time, and I had featured the identical dress in an editorial that had just come out. I remember thinking that she had chosen the outfit from the selection that I had most admired. Beyoncé's design choices on stage, in videos, and on the red carpet are all about honoring women. Even in this day of androgyny in fashion, she is never asexual and always consciously feminine in her style choices, displaying curves and female shape. It's about celebrating your feminine body, not being limited by your body form, and wearing what makes you feel good. She accepts herself just as she is. That is one of the reasons why ladies adore her.

Beyoncé has always been a supporter of diverse types of beauty taking center stage. It's something I've advocated for in my style and fashion work, from i-D to advertising campaigns and now at British Vogue. It's one of the many reasons I appreciate and respect her so much. We have a duty to fulfill. We consider ourselves fortunate to have been granted a platform, and we do not take it lightly. I grew up with beautiful women of all body types, so that was my environment, and I believe Beyoncé was comparable in that regard. Then we each developed our individual talents, but we never forgot where we came from or what our mothers, grandmothers, and aunts looked like. It's second nature to me, as I'm sure it is to Beyoncé. We don't even have to think about inclusion and diversity; it just happens. While she shows off her attributes, she is never rude, which is a crucial point. I call it the "Beyoncé Sheen," because it's when you put a degree of chic on whatever super-sexy thing you're wearing, even super-short cutoffs. It's not something you can learn; it's a natural feature that allows you to be extremely seductive while also being empowering and never being a victim.

As an outsider to American culture, I can see her Texas origins in her style. You can see the complete cheerleader concept in her, something we don't have in England. Cheerleader attire and majorette culture are both extremely American, and she channels both, especially when she wears bodysuits. She is, in reality, the bodysuit queen. She popularized that image in mainstream fashion, which is mirrored in her Ivy Park fashion line, a body-positive, youthful, and trendy fashion line that also demonstrates her influence outside of music.

Ivy Park has become a well-known trademark on the streets of London. It's definitely an athleisure brand, with joggers, bodysuits, and sports bras, but it also lives outside of that category, showcasing how she's elevated and embraced street fashion. It would have been easy for her to explore any part of the business at this point in her career and with her access to high fashion, but choosing pieces with a lower price range demonstrates her purpose of inclusiveness and her unequaled grasp of her audience. It's also worth noting that every ad since its inception in spring 2016 has included young talent, particularly women of color, in its images. The imagery illustrates her devotion to young women, but also to everyone else, to be themselves, to wear what they want, and to stand for what they want. The homosexual community adores her for this, for her commitment to standing with us, and for her glitz—the huge hair, the gorgeous makeup and figure, the whole package. She ranks among Madonna, Streisand, and Ross—all the greats. Her legacy will include being the ultimate homosexual icon.

When I travel around the world, from Africa to South America to Europe, I witness firsthand her global influence and worship. Everyone knows who she is and is motivated by her aspirational traits and the fact that she has made the world a better place simply by being in it. She will be remembered as a music star, a fashion icon, a homosexual icon, a female icon, a diversity symbol, and a philanthropist who gives back. This is all Beyoncé. We talk about trends in fashion, but she is above them. She cannot be contained in a box. To be honest, she is free to do whatever she wants.

CHAPTER 16
Beyoncé's Radiance

When and Where I Enter

I was the type of kid who never stopped moving. I discovered movement in everything. I could sit in a hotel lobby and choreograph how everyone exits the elevator and walks through the entrance, as well as how the front-desk staff performs their duties. Everything I see feels scripted, and the way I move through life feels like a dance. I finished high school at sixteen, and in Los Angeles, there were these clubs that held dancing competitions. It was the late 1980s and early 1990s, during the dawn of hip hop, and dance was central to the culture. I enjoyed the music, and all of the singers had dancers who built a name for themselves. I felt as though the clubs were my church, and I had to attend. The dance floor was where I felt the most connected to God.

We were practically inventing new dance steps and trends. Now, kids do it with each other and put it on YouTube, creating the next dance craze, but crazes were developed in clubs back then. Because I wasn't trained, I spent hours on the dance floor, which is where I obtained my training. Dancers would arrive from New York or Atlanta, and we'd all compete on the dance floor while swapping routines and learning from one another. It was truly a fantastic time.

When I went to Alvin Ailey or a dance conservatory, they never truly understood hip hop dance. Hip hop dance, on the other hand, is currently a dominant type of dance, not just for young people but also for dance organizations. It's incredible to think that it all started with hip hop artists bringing on dancers as part of the event. I never used the title choreographer to identify myself because we weren't part of the dance establishment. We were just finishing up the show. You danced with someone and made up your own routine. Dance was a natural feature of every theater production. I needed to learn how to count. I taught the lyrics or the beat of the song for years since that's where it started from for me. Now that I'm more experienced and skilled, I know how to make everything count.

Remember the Time

My first major break came when I choreographed the video for Michael Jackson's "Remember the Time." From there, it's been an incredible experience of working with artists, from those just starting out to those who want to achieve something that you know is the culmination of years of their creative progress. I choreographed Aaliyah's "Rock the Boat" and Rihanna's "Pon de Replay." The choreography of Pharrell's 24-hour "Happy" video was a breakthrough moment for both of us. Aaliyah and I were good friends both personally and professionally. She rose to prominence about the same time as Destiny's Child, so they were truly peers who admired one another. I believe Aaliyah's work influenced many people. She was a one-of-a-kind person. She had her own path, Destiny's Child had theirs, and Beyoncé built her own road out of that. When I first met Rihanna, we talked about how Aaliyah's career influenced her and inspired her to become an artist. Rihanna discussed how she would perform Aaliyah's songs.

My Introduction to Beyoncé

I've had the privilege of working with Beyoncé since Destiny's Child days. It takes a lot of persistence to break into the entertainment world, but even more fortitude to keep your status, presence, fan base, endurance, good looks, and sanity!!!!! Beyoncé is the greatest entertainer since Michael Jackson. She has been dubbed the "new Michael Jackson." Michael was a model for a whole generation of dancers, but he was also a model of work ethic for me. I was 21 years old when I choreographed "Remember the Time," and just being in the room with him, working with a perfectionist of his quality, set the tone for how I wanted to continue ahead in my career. Beyoncé possesses the same tenacity, and her work ethic is admirable. She causes everyone around her to pull up. She works quite hard. That kind of work ethic is difficult to come by. I've had performers in the room, names you've heard of, who can sing and dance, but they sit down and check their phones between takes. That is not how Beyoncé operates. Many people are unaware of the level of dedication required to attain the heights she has. Turning off everything in the outer world and focusing on who you are as a performer, as well as executing the vision that comes from the deepest part of your soul, is required.

It's her unfathomable, one-of-a-kind blend of vision, imagination, and work ethic that brings her live stage act to life. People don't realize that even the simplest dance combination signifies hours and hours and hours of doing it over and over again. It's great as a choreographer to be in a room and see an artist perfect a trick, master something that they couldn't get the day before. No matter how many times you've seen pure talent walk through the door, there's a certain way that stars carry themselves that is very unlike anything you've seen before. Artists like Rihanna, Aaliyah, and Beyoncé don't feel like they belong. They are really noticeable.

I felt Beyoncé's spirit the first time I worked with her. She had a fire in her that you don't often see in young artists. So often, you meet an artist and recognize their skill, but you think to yourself, "Okay, now we have to connect talent with business sense, work ethic, and vision." When everything comes together, you get the breakthrough—it's like, "Ah, now they've made it." Whereas with a select few, and Beyoncé is a prime example of this, you just see everything right there and right then. When you attend her presentation, you will be transported into a world of pleasure, laughing, dance, and magnificence. The lighting, gorgeous costumes, well-curated screen content, intricate stage pieces, and the woman herself all contribute to an outstanding performance. Her message of female strength lingers, and you feel like the queen you are.

Singing and Dancing Are Two Different Things

To be clear, not everyone who can sing can also dance. Some people excel at only one or the other. She's just one of those folks who truly knows dance, its language, and its complexities. People with both the talent to sing and dance at that level are quite rare. That is why everyone is so taken with that type of artist—a Michael Jackson, a Prince, a Beyoncé—because they are a unique breed.

I worked as a choreographer on the feature film Dreamgirls, in which Beyoncé played Deena Jones—she was stunning in that role. She astounded the globe not only with her singing and dancing in the film, but also with her brave acting talent. She was a perfectionist throughout rehearsals. It took hours to perfect every action, every hand gesture, every head turn, and every rotation to the camera. As a fellow Virgo, I understand how that perfectionist bug feels. She's a monster! I admired the effort—in fact, it motivated me to work even more. For months, we spent everyday together, and I frequently heard about her love of her life—now husband—Jay-Z. I'd known Jay since I was eighteen, when we went on tour with Big Daddy Kane all over the world. Jay was the emcee, and I did my thing—I danced. I was overjoyed to learn that two greats had met and liked seeing the sparkle in her eyes when she had a few days off to spend with him.

We should commend her for making her marriage a testament to the kind of authenticity that is the antithesis of most Hollywood partnerships. Spilling her heart out to the world on her sixth solo album, Lemonade, by acknowledging the flaws in her relationship only strengthened her/them. It was surprising to observe how many girl gangs there were at the last show. So many ladies came together to support Beyoncé, but they also like to do those dances together and are like, "Get me to the floor." It was wonderful to witness women having fun with each other without inhibitions. I believe she has given so many women permission to be who they are, to love who they are, and to live their lives, perfect in their flaws.

Coachella

Let's take a moment to discuss Coachella. I'm the daughter of a Tennessee State University graduate. My mother was a majorette, and my father was a musician. Beyoncé's performance, a heartfelt tribute to historically Black institutions and universities, moved me to tears. Coachella wasn't prepared for the level of authenticity she brought to her performance, from the bleacher stage design to the fireworks exploding during the horn section's crescendo, to the nonstop dance that made you want to move and sing along, to the way the songs were remixed to fit the festival crowd. It was an expertly executed stage spectacle with hundreds of moving parts.

According to Albert Einstein, "dancers are the athletes of God." When working with the greats, we push our bodies to accomplish unusual and new things, and there is creation at every level. Sometimes things go well and the creative moves come to you and everything is fine, and other times you're stuck and trying to figure out how to make it better, or something just doesn't feel right. Sometimes you have to step away from it and return to it with fresh eyes. I know Beyoncé does skeleton crews of work a lot, where you only hire a few dancers to help you ideate the piece. If there are over 100 dancers on stage at Coachella, she may do a skeleton crew with only 15 of them. Then you create a skeleton outline of where you want the piece to go, which helps you coordinate the music as well as the stage plan. From there, you just keep building and building. Orchestration has multiple layers: determining what works and what doesn't; sometimes you come back the next day and say, "That formation doesn't work." In this arrangement, these maneuvers appear superior. Or, if we relocate this bit of choreography over there, we might be able to take it." It's like emptying a clock, shaking all the components out onto the surface, and then reassembling it till it works. At that level, choreography is tweezer labor.

Making a name for oneself is easier than keeping it. To keep it going, you must continually evolve and reinvent yourself. Americans will remember Beyoncé at Coachella in the same way they remember Diana Ross performing in Central Park in the rain, Michael Jackson popping up from the scoreboards at the Super Bowl, or Josephine Baker dancing her heart out in that infamous banana dress at the Folies Bergère in Paris. Not only is Beyoncé a megastar, but she's also a mother, sister, wife, friend, and role model to many admirers who look up to her, seek guidance from her, or simply use her as inspiration to overcome whatever challenges they face in their lives. As a mother, she walks the fine line between exposing her children to too much too soon. As a sister, she is always there to support Solange, who was too young to be a member of Destiny's Child but aspired to be an entertainer in her own right. With two younger sisters, I used to make up dance routines to perform for our mother when she had company. As we grew older, our beautiful friendship allowed us to mature and go our separate ways while still supporting each other. When I see recordings of Beyoncé as a youngster, it reminds me of myself, and I credit both of our triumphs to our families' outstanding matriarchs: Ms. Tina Knowles and my mother, Khadijah Lewis. Their leadership and direction have given us the strength to persevere and have taught us life lessons that will help us reach our goals, which we will then pass on to our children.

Unpacking Her Ancestry

Beyoncé has always stood for Black Excellence. You move your butt or make a formation when she instructs you to!! She is always loyal to herself; she never dismisses culture, but instead continuously puts it to the forefront, educating others about who we are and what we do. She is continually expanding as a culture developer, pushing the boundaries and exploring uncharted ground. That's what great musicians do, and whether I'm working with Pharrell Williams or Kendrick Lamar, I'm always pushing them to be better. The creative process is thrilling. Critiquing yourself until you get it perfect, understanding when something doesn't fit in "that pocket." Questioning how performances may have an emotional impact while yet being entertaining. The unpacking and raising of Beyoncé's genealogy is one of the things you've seen in her work. Everything changed when I started taking African dance courses. The teacher would explain to us about the origins of these dances, which were eerily identical to what we did in hip hop. "This is insane," I kept thinking. We're actually performing something that comes from our ancestors without even realizing it."

Why Beyoncé's Work Feels Like Home

Dancers travel the world at the start of their careers, never leaving our hotels, eating at McDonald's all over the world, and it's quite bad. It's not just the dancers; it's any young or emerging artist. There was a shift when Beyoncé began to really open her eyes to what was around her and be exposed to art, other cultures, and dance on a global scale. You could see a new sense of ownership in her craft as she began to combine a type of dance that was true to her, even though it relied on wholly new inspiration. I've come all the way here, but for some reason, this feels like home. I need to incorporate this into my music, my world, and my art. It's basically continual change and growth for Beyoncé. Many times in an artist's life and career, I give them permission to do what they already want to do. They may feel a little terrified and cautious about it, or they may be unsure if it's the proper path to take. And I contribute to that. When an artist, such as Beyoncé, trusts her intuition and has the confidence to follow her curiosity, magic happens. We react to Beyoncé the way we do because we are witnessing her development, which is rare—and amazing.

CHAPTER 17
Because Beyoncé

It doesn't matter what you want to know about her: her life, her music, or her profession. Ultimately, the answer is always "Because Beyonc"é." I was 23 when I first heard of her. That was 20 years ago, when I was the program director of one of Sacramento's largest radio stations. They were making young music and looked like what was going on in the clubs and on the street at the time. But what I liked and noticed the most about Beyoncé was that she wasn't trying to be soft like some of the other late-nineties acts. With a record that was both hip hop and mainstream, she was breaking new ground. And, of course, it featured a lot of various aspects, which has always been one of her music's strengths. Above all, that was a strong record, and Beyoncé sounded strong on it. You wished for more of that music, and especially more of her.

Then, in 1999, she gave us a lot more. That's when the songs started getting stronger, with The Writing's on the Wall album and songs like "Bills, Bills, Bills," "Bug A Boo," "Jumpin', Jumpin'," and "Say My Name." That was also the point at which it became absolutely evident that Beyoncé would embrace the daring while lyrically tapping into whatever was going culturally and was authentic. Cute and meek are not her characteristics. And, to be honest, how can Beyoncé be cute or timid as an adult? She can't help but sound aggressive while also seductive when she speaks. That is a unique skill. Consider her delivery. Listening to Beyoncé's records, it's as if she's performing in front of you. She is the official record holder. Only the greats, such as Tina Turner, are capable of doing so. In fact, I see a lot of Tina Turner in Beyoncé—the way she has her legs out, her enthusiasm onstage—as do many others.

There is a way in songs like "Apesh*t" when she says, "suck my dick" or as "King Bey" where she incorporates a masculine demeanor, although it's prevalent with street females and around-the-way gals. It's designed to be insulting. It's intended to be condescending. It's supposed to be all of that. It's entertaining. It's just nonsense. I believe that when she's Beyoncé, the badass, it reminds women that she's still herself despite being a mother of three children. Despite being one of the most renowned ladies on the planet, she can be exactly like them and not care. Yes, I have all this money and I don't have to fuck with people who don't understand our shit.

Beats 1 has been a fantastic education in what music is and how it is perceived around the world. I began working there on the first day it was operational in June 2015. I've spent my entire career in radio, but I never anticipated that I'd be hosting a radio show that would be heard in over 100 countries, with simultaneous streaming—so many people listening to the same songs at the same time in every time zone on the planet. My goal is to locate and deliver engaging stuff to individuals. I consider myself as a conduit, a sort of middleman if you will. A DJ's role is to offer music in a consumable and accessible manner while also providing context. What I've learned the most in this capacity is the international power of hip hop.

I can't help but observe Beyoncé's diverse fan base, both locally and globally. Beyoncé. Her name reflects her Creole origin, which has apparent French ties through slavery, Africa, and so on. Then you see her love for Paris, which is completely mutual. She, like that city, is a cultural hotspot. People believe that the first large movement of African Americans to Paris came with Josephine Baker and then the Harlem Renaissance, but it actually dates back to the Louisiana Purchase in 1803. And Louisiana transports you right back to Beyoncé's Creole roots. Paris has served as a haven for numerous African American artists. Paris is beautiful, yet it is quite classy. It's like any other place, with its rich and poor, as well as the entirely disenfranchised.

Beyoncé enters a room and never leaves her Blackness behind, despite the fact that she could be a celebrity. She did that while filming "Apesh*t" at the Louvre. Black people are nearly all shown as slaves in the Louvre. The gold in Paris's streets is stolen from Africa. The obelisks and pyramid iconography are both African. Paris has robbed Africa. The folks who built it were kidnapped from Africa. The art in the Louvre, on the other hand, only depicts Black people as possessions. Beyoncé and Jay are a living art exhibit of

Blackness and African-ness, hence I assume she shot that video in the Louvre. They made that remark into a music video that will live on in perpetuity.

Still, it appears that Beyoncé is not for everyone. As an example, she has yet to win a Grammy for Album of the Year. How many times do we need to be reminded of America's cultural understanding imbalance? She amassed massive fame across numerous tribes and produced critically acclaimed albums, yet she has yet to win a Grammy for Album of the Year. But when it comes to the Grammys, the folks who have voting power aren't paying attention to popular media or mainstream music consumption; they're simply voting based on what they know.

Lemonade has songs from a variety of genres. It was released in a unique manner. It was innovative in many respects, and as we see in politics, the new is difficult. That being said, I feel that if the album had been created by someone white, those fresh concepts would have been more widely accepted. And now consider what they did to Jay-Z at the 2018 Grammys when he published his record on Tidal. Do these voters have a problem with Jay and Bey directing their own fate and the release of their music in this manner?

Fortunately, Beyoncé's capacity to fight is one of her other amazing strengths. Life knocks her down, but she gets back up and wins. So, without a doubt, the shelf lacking an Album of the Year Grammy provides her a cause to keep working and us a reason to keep in touch with her. And she will, and we—her followers, particularly those who have grown up with her—will be a part of it, as we always have been. Beyoncé has opened up about her life to us. Her admirers have grown up with her in this day and age of openness. That's a lot of life to live in public, and we're grateful for her superpowers of bravery and humility, which allowed us to bear witness. We trust and admire Beyoncé because she has spent decades cultivating a close relationship with her followers. We live in a country that is polarized. Though she isn't on a soapbox, Beyoncé isn't hesitant to speak out through her music and actions. She has shown tremendous support for President Barack Obama and Michelle Obama.

She has shown support for anyone speaking out against police violence. She has expressed support for Colin Kaepernick. She has repeatedly used Black Panther symbols to indicate her support for the Black Nationalist cause. And Black people understand the danger. On the 50th anniversary of the Black Panthers, a group that was once viewed as a threat to the American way of life by the FBI, Beyoncé walked out at the greatest broadcast event ever, lifted her fist in the air, and sported an afro to pay tribute. And to the naysayers who sprang up to oppose her: Black people know exactly what people were attempting to do to discredit her. Detractors were attempting to frame and build a narrative in which she was either problematic or insulting to American society. They chastised her for paying homage to people from similar communities to her own, and for honoring a community that had to fight and lead the way for Black people to be respected by police enforcement and the government.

In our opinion, for one of the biggest stars on the planet to walk out and raise her fist in the air is to jeopardize everything. Another of her superpowers is that she placed herself in danger for all of us. Consider how many times we've witnessed a Black celebrity stand up for oppressed people, particularly Black people, and be attacked, ostracized, or both. Colin Kaepernick is experiencing this right now—he is unable to find work. However, because Beyoncé is self-made and works for herself, she is largely impervious to being brought down. Few Black people in America are aware of their untouchability.

The majority of us have always worked for someone else. We're expendable if we fall out of line or do anything unpopular. But you won't be able to get rid of Beyoncé. Nobody can stop Beyoncé from communicating with her followers and releasing songs. She makes music videos in the way she sees fit. She chooses how to release her songs. Beyoncé represents a beautiful, Black, strong woman all around the world. She denotes strength. She is self-made and prosperous. I am a Beyhive member with pride. I admire her work ethic and devotion, as well as the way she stands her ground. I admire her for raising my four-year-old daughter. She will always have not only Beyoncé's discography, but also all of the visual material and live performances of someone who overcame all odds to become an icon and whose complexion and hair texture are identical to hers. When you can see yourself in someone else, it's a gift. Whatever angle you take on this diva, one thing remains constant: "Because Beyoncé."

CHAPTER 18
King Bey

"Get off my dick." I laughed out loud the first time I heard this sentence in "Apesh*t." The cockiness (all puns intended) of the demand while discussing her pricey materials and habits and having the power to make someone famous after only one night with her delighted me in both its honesty and its well-earned arrogance. There was not a single falsehood in her assertions about her money and celebrity. Any sense of humility or modesty is missing from this song, particularly her lines and chorus. She truly embraces a confidence that few Black women can openly express without paying a high price. I was taken aback by her unwavering and shameless confidence.

"Apesh*t" was far from Beyoncé's first time singing or rapping about her prowess or commanding others to accept her grind and successes. The first single from her joint album with her husband and frequent collaborator, Jay-Z, simply displays a performative boldness she developed in the 1990s and began flaunting in the 2010s: King Bey. Beyoncé's shit-talking, boastful, and aggressive character is one of the most intriguing and possibly surprising aspects in her illustrious 20-plus-year career. She'd been bootylicious, a diva, and even a Queen—but the birth and evolution of King Bey heralded the beginning of a new chapter in her legendary career. Everything Is Love is a body of work in which Beyoncé, as King Bey, establishes a distinct spot within hip hop as a fully fledged performing identity.

Hip hop, particularly Southern hip hop, has played and continues to play an important influence in Beyoncé's visual, auditory, style, and dance aesthetics throughout her career. Beyoncé's link to hip hop is apparent, whether she collaborated with Wyclef Jean on the remix to Destiny's Child's first hit or appeared in a Willie D video. There has never been a time in Beyoncé's career when she has not been identified with hip hop music culture. When her first girl group, ladies Tyme, landed a slot on the "greatest talent competition show ever," Star Search, in 1993, host Ed McMahon referred to the six young Black ladies as a "hip hop, rappin' group." Destiny's Child's debut is closely related to hip hop as well. Not only did their first video from their debut album involve rapper-producer Wyclef Jean, but they also used a hip hop-influenced remix of "No, No, No" to expose themselves to a national audience.

A hip hop mainstay, particularly in the 1990s, the remix often outperforms the original in popularity. "No, No, No" was no different. Beyoncé took the lead, riding what Wyclef referred to in the music video as a "phat beat for the clubs." The remix of the soulful track featured an almost rap-singing tone to her delivery, which became a defining part of both Destiny's Child's and Beyoncé's vocal performances. Her quick singing, unusual phrasing, and smooth transitions between breathy, soulful notes and percussive and harsh vocal delivery distinguish her as one of the most distinctive voices in modern pop music. Beyoncé is a singer who draws on soul, R&B, and pop traditions, but her unwavering love of hip hop also contributes to her distinct style.

Destiny's Child never shied away from the impact of hip hop in their production or style, so it's no surprise that when Beyoncé momentarily split from the group, hip hop played an important role in her solo efforts. She recorded the main single, "Work It Out," for the soundtrack of her film Austin Powers in Goldmember before releasing her first album in 2003. Months later, the first single from the soundtrack of another of her films, Fighting Temptations, with female rappers Missy Elliott, MC Lyte, and Free, was released. Beyoncé finished the year with a guest appearance on Jay-Z's (then-rumored) tune "'03 Bonnie & Clyde." The ride-or-die track peaked at number four on the Billboard Hot 100, fueling speculation of a post-Destiny's Child Beyoncé album.

On June 24, 2003, Beyoncé reaffirmed her love of hip hop by releasing "Crazy in Love," the first single off her debut solo album, Dangerously in Love, featuring Jay-Z. Beyoncé's lighthearted pop tune with a hip hop twist catapulted her into the musical stratosphere, where she remains. Dangerously in Love is one of the more R&B-influenced and established entries in her six-album catalog, with two collaborations with Jay-Z as well as features from rap singers Missy Elliott and Big Boi. Elliott, as well as hip hop and R&B producers

Rich Harrison and Scott Storch, were instrumental in establishing the sound of Beyoncé's debut album. Dangerously in Love became a critically acclaimed and commercially successful album, earning Knowles five Grammys, a Billboard Music Award, and other nominations. She bet on soul and hip hop to distinguish her pop songs from the competition. She was victorious.

Beyoncé's celebrity and fandom grew with each album, tour, and broadcast performance, as did her unashamed love and respect for hip hop collaborations. When Destiny's Child reunited in 2004, one of their most memorable and commercially successful tracks from their previous album, Destiny Fulfilled, was "Soldier." Beyoncé gradually introduced the world to her alter ego, Sasha Fierce, after her first handful of solo ventures. Beyoncé rose to prominence as Sasha, a sassy diva with a large ego and Black female attitude. Beyoncé's popularity soared, and so did her monikers. Each of Beyoncé's monikers—Queen Bey, Yoncé, or Baddie Bey—had a unique connotation. Many of the monikers played with hip hop posturing and the kind of bravado that is commonly associated with rap performers. The most recent addition to the list, King Bey, reflects both Bey's experience with hip hop and her more recent shift toward rapping and rap bravado as a space for expression, not merely collaboration.

In 2013, her voice and manner were heavily influenced by the creation of King Bey. It was called "Bow Down/I Been On." The track immediately enticed and disgusted me. While many praised her rap-singing innovation, the chopped and screwed second verse, and the considerably more explicit lyrics, the backlash to her percussive insistence that "bitches bow down" was equally swift. After stating that girls rule the world, many people were surprised when Beyoncé released a song in which she brags about asking her crew to "smack that trick." I liked Beyoncé before this song, but I became a fan when it came out.

While Queen Bey demanded that bitches bend down, it was King Bey who reminisced about her childhood in Houston and wondered about stunting in her "gold everything." Her memories of wearing dookie braids and confessing to sneaking to listen to UGK are enlivened by her use of chopped and screwed, a sound pioneered by the late DJ Screw in Houston in the late 1980s and early 1990s. It's a performance on her hometown and her complicated relationship with her city's working-class Black culture as a middle-class African American child and teenager. As Regina Bradley points out in "I Been On (Ratchet)," Beyoncé provides a persona on this track. Initially known as Baddie Bey, this character serves as an introduction and formative forerunner to King Bey.

Knowles-Carter reworked "Bow Down/I Been On" into "Flawless," a women's liberation anthem for Beyoncé's seminal self-titled visual album. Queen Bey returned with a track featuring a sample of famed novelist Chimamanda Ngozi Adichie's TED Talk on feminism, as well as a handful of excellent catchphrases for the decade. The cultural significance of the phrase "I woke up like this" cannot be emphasized. Beyoncé took a song that many condemned for its anti-feminist tone and substance and turned it into a defining anthem. With "Flawless," Queen Bey established herself as a significant figure in pop culture feminism. Although the song and visual album were widely associated with Queen Bey, it was the King Bey ethos—one profoundly rooted in daring and self-assurance—that propelled Beyoncé's rebuttal to her detractors via the reworking of "Bow Down/I Been On." She was not backing down or downplaying her claims to be pop cultural royalty.

King Bey made a comeback on Lemonade, her aesthetically striking and sonically diverse solo album. In one of the most humorous yet honest songs about cheating and being fed up with her partner, she raps, "suck on my balls, pause." This is a very hip hop moment. Numerous hip hop singers utilize "suck my dick" and other colloquial expressions for fellatio to denigrate, mock, or discard the object of their rage. The mention of balls or, subsequently, her "dick" isn't what makes her King Bey. When she dabbles in hip hop's particular lexicon, she reveals herself as King Bey. "Suck on my balls" or "get off my dick" could be viewed as Beyoncé repeating some of hip hop's toxic, misogynist, homophobic, and sexist terminology. While that is a true criticism, it is also feasible to see this as Beyoncé claiming a throne in hip hop, a music genre dominated by men. She enters the area as both King and Queen Bey, which her husband, one of the greatest rappers of all time, cannot do. Everything Is Love is Beyoncé's most overtly hip hop project to date. It brings together Queen and King Bey.

Her hip hop bravado is prominent in some of the most memorable moments. Beyoncé, whether singing "I can do anything" or "I'm Malcolm X," has begun a new chapter in her illustrious career, which is constantly evolving. More than any of her other alter personalities or identities, King Bey displays Beyoncé's passion for hip hop. Hip hop is integrated into practically every part of this era of her career, from the posturing to the lyrical delivery. Beyoncé swings fluidly between her numerous characters in her most recent tour, On the Run II, but it is King Bey who concludes the event. She ends it by riding the beat smoothly on "Apesh*t." Beyoncé walks off the stage knowing she reigns over both a Queendom and a Kingdom. There is no precedent in mainstream culture for an artist being referred to as both King and Queen. She defies the rules, which only adds to her hip hop confidence. Beyoncé's path to icon hood is one of self-transformation as a performer. Her resistance to become complacent or fixed as an entertainer, artist, and collaborator adds considerably to her remarkable success. Beyoncé is primarily competing with herself at this time, so why not be both King and Queen?

CHAPTER 19
Beyoncé's Southern Origins and References

My dismal feelings are helped by music, but Beyoncé was not on my playlist or on my radar when she launched her solo career the year I turned 25. I had already left the rural vistas of Chatham County, North Carolina, for the Florida peninsula. Leaving had felt like an escape and a rescue because my greatest worry had been shrinking myself to the point of being engulfed by the hollowness of my hometown. My next home brought me from the old South to the deep South. When I traveled up from Tampa, through Tallahassee, Dothan, Montgomery, and Tuscaloosa, Alabama felt eerily familiar. Alabama was to be a reprieve, a place for me to remake myself, settle into my independence, learn how to make a living on my own, and create a life grander than I had previously imagined.

Beyoncé has released two more albums and numerous anthems by that point. Beyoncé was already a household name, exoticized rather than ghettoized by her physical attractiveness and crossover appeal. Her carefully cultivated public character was never without a nod to her humble background in Houston. Beyoncé, like me, lived close to home, metaphorically if not literally, and was always reppin. The Southern drawl in her speaking voice, the Houstonian accent in her spoken words on tracks, her collaboration with down South hip hop heads like Andre 3000, Bun B, and Slim Thug, and the visual and iconic imagery of southscapes she offered in music videos were all obvious sonic signifiers of the south. Shout-outs and subtle Southern innuendos have always been prominent in her work, but on her fifth and eponymous album, she seemed to shift from "repping" to embodying where she was from.

While Beyoncé's cultural currency had always transcended the South, she doubled down on her Southern sound in 2013, following the internet release of "Bow Down/I Been On," with an embrace of dirty South/trap music as a way of acknowledging and owning her full country self—complications, contradictions, and all. Beyoncé reintroduced herself as someone who was not only from the South, but who related with the South—and its associated and working-class aesthetics—in that song, which was ultimately released as the first section of "Flawless" on her self-titled album. The South, whether urban or rural, is frequently linked with impoverished areas, rurality, backward thinking, and conservative religion. There is also the assumption that the majority of Southerners are white. Beyoncé defies negative assumptions by presenting the South as a prominent character in her art rather than allowing it to fade into the background. Her graphic collages of Black bodies in diverse hues and circumstances blend opulence with deficiency like sugar syrup in sweet tea.

Instead of categorizing Blackness in the South, she combines it—young and old, city and country, holy and secular, cis and trans, light skinned and dark, heterosexual and queer, public and private, but all Black—inviting her global audience to a new way of seeing and understanding American Southern culture. While Beyoncé grew up in a traditional, cis-het home in a middle-class neighborhood, she is still able to access and signify ratchetness (behavior associated with the ghettoization of Black womanhood) and respectability—simultaneously, and without the threat or impression of co-optation or appropriation.

She exemplifies ratchet respectability, a political combination of ratchetness and respectability that seeks to debunk some preconceptions (about Black women) while embracing others. Beyoncé teased her sixth studio album, Lemonade, with the surprise release of "Formation," a song and video that embraced stereotypical perceptions of the South by highlighting them.

Messy Mya and Big Freedia lend their Louisiana-tinged voices to the song and video. Their phrases and distinct accents are inadvertently authentic, lending validity to the song's goal to be(come) a Southern anthem. Beyoncé's purpose is to foreground and honor Southern Black culture and her Southern Black lineage, as evidenced by the refrain, which reminds us where her parents are from and where she was raised.

She also manages to locate tastes in soul cuisine, baby hair, Negro nostrils, and hot sauce as not just Black, but Southern Black.

Beyoncé is juxtaposed against Black women with colored weaves in a beauty supply store, scenes from a Black church and Black spirituality, representations of Southern goth, an all-Black marching band, a Black man wearing a cowboy hat on a horse, and Black women dressed in white holding hand fans as we shift from weatherworn homes drowned by floodwaters to a group of Black women twerking. Beyoncé insisted with the inclusion of a traditional country song on Lemonade that ownership of country music is not limited to white people in Nashville or Black males in the dirty South. "Daddy Lessons," a song about a bad father giving his daughter lessons about "men like him," has all the trappings of a country song, including straightforward narration and references to evangelical Christianity, weapons, and relationships.

Despite the song's success, which included an invitation for Beyoncé to perform at the Country Music Awards in 2016, it was rejected by the Recording Academy's country music committee, making her ineligible for a Grammy award nomination in the country music categories—an apparent rejection of her efforts to portray herself or her brand as country. Her move into country music drew criticism from some (who thought it wasn't "country enough") and praise from others (who said it was "classic country"). Regardless of the disagreements, the song, which was later performed by the country group Dixie Chicks, demonstrates Beyoncé's artistry traverses boundaries and genres—and that Bey's Southern roots and references are vast enough to incorporate handclaps and two-steps.

Lemonade was a tribute to Black women as well as an ode to the South. Beyoncé developed a visually striking depiction of the South with a look that centered on how we view ourselves rather than how we are regarded by others by prioritizing and discovering the beauty in settings and bodies that are frequently erased or rendered ugly in mainstream media. By sharing Black women's tales that centered rather than excluded them, this Southern subjectivity provided visibility and recognition. Lemonade was an uncompromising Black-woman-centered and focused initiative, a personalized open letter to our resilience, and an invitation to self-love and acceptance—it tapped the rural origins of Blackness and the resonance of Black women's intergenerational, diasporic experiences.

Beyoncé poured metaphorical Lemonade in a see-through pitcher, like a see-through picture, and made me feel vulnerable, but visible—a visibility that reverberated throughout the Black community, but especially among those of us who live in the South, grew up in the South, and recognized our mothers, grandmothers, and sisters in the story line. She employed the camera lens to capture the essence of the Black experience by emphasizing elements that are otherwise unappealing. Every still image was powerful. Beyoncé crossed many areas while playing with dual identities, including huge open fields, decaying ghettos, plantation mansions, and parking lots. She investigated physical space and landscapes, placing the South as more than urban or concrete, but also rural and red mud.

Lemonade's reclamation of the South was compatible with recent movements in her work toward Blackness, feminism, and social justice activism—all of which present in the visual album. She reaffirms and reconciles her Southern identity in the tradition of blues women, Black feminists, and foremothers, all of whom have legacies long buried in Southern soil. The South's residue and legacies will definitely remain crucial to Beyoncé's work, but Lemonade was something special, something extraordinary. It reawakened my desire to actively anchor my art in my Southern heritage. It reminded me of how important it is to know who we are, where we came from, and where we belong. Beyoncé's acceptance of Black womanhood infused with Southerness served as a reminder that she sees us and is one of us.

CHAPTER 20
B & V: A Love Letter

It was April 2004—before Lemonade, Blue, Rumi, or Sir. In truth, the future Mrs. Carter was still Beyoncé Knowles at the time, and while Bey was huge, her hive, and she, weren't fully grown. She was 22, madly in love with her then-boyfriend Jay-Z, and had already spent more than half her life acting her heart out. She was the age she would have been graduating from college if she had taken a more traditional route. But there was nothing traditional about Beyoncé Giselle Knowles—not her name, her beauty (or much-touted booty), or her extraordinary talent. When it came to work, she was meticulous, and excellence was her default setting. Despite her polite and ladylike demeanor in interviews, it was easy to mistake her fiery ambition for a desire to please. In fact, it was simple to dismiss her entirely back then. Her quirks—the deep-throated, funny laugh and her inability to shake that Houston accent—kept her authentic, even vulnerable, and made you want to hug her. But her hungry gaze and the meticulous manner in which she handled everything gave her away. Beyoncé was drawing near-sellout crowds as she tested the solo waters in the aftermath of her debut album, Dangerously in Love, at the end of a two-year break from Destiny's Child. When it was released in 2003, it debuted at No. 1 on the Billboard 200 albums list, selling 300,000 copies in its first week.

Despite the group's global popularity and her rising comfort level murdering onstage without her sidekicks Kelly Rowland and Michelle Williams, Beyoncé looked uneasy about parting ways with them. Having grown up with these girls, whom she still refers to as sisters, the generally collected ingénue would battle not to cry when asked about leaving them. Beyoncé, managed by her father, Mathew, dressed by her mother, Tina, and raised alongside Rowland and her baby sister, Solange, recognized Destiny's Child as a force with a stack of Grammys and a devoted female following. It was extremely difficult to say goodbye because it was also a family business where the family was tight and business was thriving. But mastering difficult things, especially the material that stars are built of, was Beyoncé's chosen way of life.

Her Houston-based female group bounced back quickly after losing on TV's Star Search in 1993, when a prepubescent Beyoncé took the lead on vocals but didn't quite shine. When I first saw the clip at the start of her 2013 Flawless video, I bowed my head in admiration. The irony was smart, but her willingness to admit her own early failure was part of what earned her a pedestal—a throne, in fact—in a stratosphere all her own. In 1993, I was a new magazine editor, working at Black Enterprise with my spouse and in-laws. I'd learned a thing or two about juggling work and family, just like young Bey. But, as a first-time mother, I had no idea how drastically my life was about to change. My baby girl, born with a penetrating gaze and a headful of jet hair, looked so much like me that my adoring parents began calling her by my name. Veronica Nicole Graves, on the other hand, was completely unique from the start. She had an all-seeing, all-knowing quality that gave me pause even before she could walk or talk. The elders would describe it as "an old soul," but it was more than that. I prayed, looking into her eyes as I held her tight, that I would know and be enough to lead her through. I'd never felt so powerful, or so insignificant.

We soon found our groove, and it had its own sweet soundtrack crooned straight from the heart by me: lullabies and kiddie tunes like "The Wheels on the Bus" and "You Are My Sunshine"; the Charlie Chaplin-penned heartbreaker "Smile" (best covered in my shameless opinion by my grandfather, Nat King Cole); anything off the original Broadway album from The Wiz or the movie Waiting to Exhale ("Shoop-Shoop," anyone? We'd be jammin' in the car, exchanging grins in the rearview mirror while Veronica kicked in her car seat and I cranked up the music to amp up our happiness. Stevie, Luther, Chaka, Mariah, and lots of TLC jammed with Sade, Whitney, Yolanda Adams, and my aunt, Sweetie, aka Natalie Cole. Veronica's black eyes danced every time I sang, as if to indicate that all the rest may come and go as long as she had me.

Veronica grew into her knowledge and love of the music I fed her, and Beyoncé morphed from a shy girl who loved the stage to a burgeoning powerhouse who had learned to dominate it as I grew into parenthood. I saw her rise from simple skill to natural force with mild interest. Meanwhile, I marveled as my baby girl grew into her own person, with her own musical choices and a fan who would respect Beyoncé in a manner that I had never revered anyone before.

Veronica was nine years old when Dangerously in Love was released, the same age Beyoncé was when host Ed McMahon mispronounced her name on Star Search. (Imagine being unable to utter her name!) To commemorate my first born's first double-digit birthday, I decided to surprise her with a night out at her first major concert. The Verizon Ladies First Tour visit at Madison Square Garden provided the ideal ticket at the perfect time. It included a triad of A-list performers, including Missy Elliott, Alicia Keys, and Beyoncé as the closer. Tamia was scheduled to appear as a "special guest" at the start of the four-hour show. It was a big event, and not just because of the fantastic title. Never before have three of the top female R&B or hip hop performers (that's Billboard code for Black) shared a single bill. In comparison to the extremely successful, very white, all-female summer music festival of the late 1990s, the music press nicknamed Ladies First the "urban Lilith Fair."

Veronica liked Alicia and played the piano. I'd often hear her from the living room, trying to peck out the notes to "Fallin'" or "If I Ain't Got You" instead of practicing. I was (and still am) a big Missy fan, but I wasn't ready to hear my fourth grader chirping "Get Ur Freak On," so I kept most of Missy's singles on repeat. All that mattered for one night was that Veronica was going to see Beyoncé live! To be honest, I was conflicted about supporting my impressionable small girl's Beyoncéssion at first. Music might be one of the many speed traps that come with motherhood. Granted, Beyoncé was dubbed the "sweetheart of hip hop," but "Bootylicious" was released around the same time as most of Missy's tracks.

Beyoncé never once betrayed her parents or her roots in her desire for freedom. She had no appetite for haterade or competitive drama in her drive for success. (Her father bore the brunt of Destiny's Child turmoil, while Bey cleverly avoided any diva/mean-girl drama.) Drugs, alcohol, or rehab? Nope, and any overt eroticism kept firmly in the realm of performance art. Her tenacity appeared to blossom as she grew older. Despite her desire to own the future of music,

Beyoncé frequently paid homage to its heritage, demonstrating a respect for her royal forefathers that plainly flowed both ways. Beyoncé was presented by none other than the King of Pop's three children at a Michael Jackson tribute performance two years after his death. Before Beyoncé embarked into a mind-blowing performance of the Jackson Five classic "I Wanna Be Where You Are," Paris Jackson stated solemnly: "She carries the torch lit by our father." After performing with Bey at the 2015 Grammys, Tina Turner (dubbed the Queen of Rock) said she "felt proud" that Bey had "taken on the memory of my life in a really positive way." Even Prince (about whom Stevie Wonder famously declared, "If Michael Jackson was the King of Pop, Prince should be the Emperor") admired Bey enough to join her onstage at the Grammys for a stunning rendition of "Purple Rain." When asked which "young divas" she endorsed in 2013, Natalie Cole labeled Beyoncé "the new Madonna." Girls want to look like her, dress like her, and she might have a big impact." She noted that Bey was "nice," and "definitely not a 'diva'" in the usual sense, despite the fact that her great-niece, Veronica, was one of those females.

Perhaps not, but Bey was tough. She took unwarranted and extremely visible risks, pushing the boundaries of her talents and skills even when the results were mixed (we nearly wore out The Fighting Temptations DVD in our house). She never played it safe, became defensive, or cowered in the face of criticism. She just received additional guidance and took the next important step. Her perfectionism, which is such a prevalent trap for girls and women, made me think. However, it was clear that her zero tolerance for compromise was simply baked into her desire to be the best, and that it was as much about satisfying herself as it was about pleasing anybody else. That, I concluded, made her a very decent role model for my kid or anyone, even myself. So I went ahead and bought the Ladies First tickets, and we've never looked back. Veronica, who had been giddy with excitement on the walk to the Garden, became apprehensive as we approached our seats. The crowded auditorium, along with her anxiety about what to anticipate, had made her wary and quiet. Veronica was overjoyed by the time Tamia, Missy, and Alicia concluded their sets.

Sean When "Puffy" Combs walked by, she gawked and giggled, but when Beyoncé appeared, it was as if Puffy went poof. There. She. Was. sat on a gilded platform being carried through the crowd by four shirtless, muscular men. As she flung petals to her shouting followers, small sparkles of light flashed off her skimpy 22-karat outfit. "If Muhammad Ali had been at Madison Square Garden Monday night, no doubt he would've found something to pound like a drum as he yelled, 'The champ is here!'" said Shaheem Reid of MTV News. 'The champion has arrived!' That's exactly the vibe Beyoncé exuded as she began her last set." Veronica followed Bey with her entire body as she floated by us. She sat up taller, pushed her narrow shoulders back, slid to the edge of her seat, and peered in, captivated, thrilled. Starstruck.

I was equally captivated by each of them. Beyoncé departed her majestic perch, her honey-spun locks flowing, and the crowd's cheers collided with the thundering intro of "Baby Boy," as if in slow motion. But she took off from the moment her metallic heels touched the stage, throwing hair, sequined hips, and rich, swift voice as if her life depended on it and she might never get another chance. Alicia had been named the show's standout by several critics, but Beyoncé was clearly in her element at the Garden that night. Her soaring, searing vocals propelled "Me, Myself, and I" to unexpected heights, and when Jay-Z joined her for their duet on "Crazy in Love," there was no mistaking their killer chemistry, or the fact that we were witnessing real-time testimony when she sang, "You got me sprung, and I don't care who sees, 'cause, baby, you got me, you got me so crazy." (Me and V went insane as well; to this day, I defy anyone to sit still when they hear the song.) When Rowland and Williams arrived for a medley of Destiny's Child hits, the crowd erupted, and when Bey, Kelly, and Michelle raised their fists for their rebellious hymn, "Survivor," 20,000 others did as well. For a brief period, the music stopped and only this thunderous chant echoed across the arena:

I'm a survivor
I'm gonna make it
I will survive
Keep on survivin'

My throat choked as I flashed back to my own mother and I, singing Aretha Franklin's "Respect" at the top of our lungs as we loaded the dishwasher and my father sat in the next room, my face solemn, her slim arm outstretched in the air like an upside-down exclamation mark. Years would pass before I discovered that my mother sang when she was joyful and when she was angry. "Respect" was at the top of her I'm-pissed hit parade, and she'd always belt it out within audible range of my father.

I still can't listen to the song without thinking of my mum and her musical line in the sand. When she sang it, she assumed a posture of defiance and tenacity, similar to the one that "Survivor" inspired in women of all ages decades later. As a child, I enjoyed singing "Respect" with my mother (and Queen Aretha!) but was unsure what it meant and was too shy to ask. I grinned as I saw Veronica chant with her fist up high, seeing history repeat itself. Survivor? She was completely unaware. Beyoncé shouted out the lines she helped create, which were captured in close-up on a big screen above the stage. Her expression was similar to my child's, as she pretended to be tough, mature, and certain. I recognized her expression; in fact, I was quite familiar with it. I wore it even in my forties, as a published novelist with a career, spouse, mortgage, and a wonderful son to nurture alongside my daughter. It's a mask that says, "I'm ready," even when you aren't; even when you're unsure, hurt, or terrified. Even if you're chanting "R-E-S-P-E-C-T" at the top of your lungs, deceiving your youngster into thinking you're in a good mood when all you want to do is cry. Life seems to spiral out from that Ladies First moment, changing completely and quickly.

When Beyoncé shocked the music business and the world in 2016 with the surprise release of her visual album, Lemonade, she was a 35-year-old singer, wife, and mother who had earned each of those titles after enduring a lot. She, too, was eager to share. She performed fewer interviews (a part of the business she never appeared to enjoy) and felt far less need for them now that she had complete control of herself, her immense influence, and her increasing money. She expertly controlled the most important thing each of us has—her own narrative—by crafting her own answers to her own questions and selectively releasing them on her own terms.

That gentle femininity that had drawn her to the press and her followers early on had developed like her voice—riper, richer, and stronger as she documented and projected it through her own lens. Although journalists occasionally referred to Sasha Fierce, Bey no longer needed alternate identities. She showed up as herself, completely integrated, complex, mature, and unapologetic. She had won and endured enough to properly claim hip hop's throne ("Bow down, bitches!"), employing every new media tool available to amplify the power that her ability, creativity, fortune, and, yes, choice of a spouse had already gained her. Veronica was 22 at the time, the same age B had been at her first solo show, and she hadn't missed a tour since. Veronica was as front and center as she could be, even when she had to mobilize her own network (and cash) to get there—sometimes traveling to other states and occasionally seeing the same show more than once. Aunt Sweetie was devastated when she learned that V had gotten a nicer section at the Mrs. Carter concert in Brooklyn than she had. Natalie examined the top tiers as she dialed Veronica, who swiftly directed her to the center of the floor, where she stood on her tippy toes and waved until Natalie found her and fell out laughing. V had not only stood in line for hours to get onto the floor, but she had also attended the same show the night before.

Veronica's Uncle Tommy got her the greatest tickets she'd ever had to the Formation World Tour at New York's Citi Field as a graduation gift. Veronica stood so close to the stage that she could almost touch it as B and her magnificent all-girl army stomped through Freedom. Her second goal of the night? She brought her hesitant brother, Carter, and eventually persuaded him to become a B-keeper as well. That event was a high point in a difficult transitional summer. Veronica would have moved out of our house, out of New York, and into her first real job and apartment by the conclusion. She felt powerful at moments, but sometimes afraid and small. Sweetie had died—too young—a few months previously, after a gallant struggle with illness, and loss weighed heavy in the air. Whatever V was experiencing, Bey had a song to help her get through it.

Of course, I was there as well, but mothers and daughters don't always hear, see, or pay attention to each other, and independence isn't easy to give or gain. Even when we were in different states (or states of mind) at the time, I'd occasionally get a text or call out of nowhere, overflowing with the latest news from the queen hive. Connecting over Beyoncé's journey has become an extension of ours.

Perhaps Beyoncé remembers the Ladies First Tour as a glittering period when life was uncomplicated, even as she made her own first daring, life-altering actions. She was already a celebrity. That would have sufficed for most people. But Bey is still hungry; you can sense it in her eyes. Veronica has adopted that look as well. I continue to monitor them both with the same mix of worry and admiration that I experienced that night, wondering what they'll do next, how they'll utilize their voices, and what they may have to survive to make their dreams come true. Life is difficult for powerful women, and it is even more difficult for people of color, even in a world awash in followers and fans. As I watch, smiling, on the edge of my seat, my Queen Bey music blasting for the ride, captivated, delighted, I applaud and pray for us all, but especially for Veronica. Starstruck.

Printed in Great Britain
by Amazon